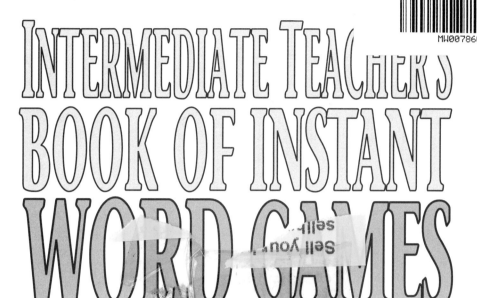

INTERMEDIATE TEACHER'S BOOK OF INSTANT WORD GAMES

Over 200 Ready-to-Use Games and Activities
for Any Basal or Whole Language Program!

JUDIE L.H. STROUF

**THE CENTER FOR APPLIED
RESEARCH IN EDUCATION**
West Nyack, New York 10994

Library of Congress Cataloging-in-Publication Data

Strouf, Judie L. H.
    Intermediate teacher's book of instant word games / Judie L. H.
  Strouf.
        p.   cm.
      ISBN 0-87628-458-6 (S)—ISBN 0-87628-459-4 (P)
      1. Educational games.   2. Word games.   3. Puzzles.   4. Language
  arts (Elementary)   5. Education, Elementary—Activity programs.
  I. Title.
  LB1029.G3.S77   1996   95-26116
  371.3′078—dc20   CIP

Printed in the United States of America

10   9   8   7   6   5   4   3   2   10   9   8   7   6   5   4   3   2   1   (pbk)

Clip Art courtesy of Dover Clip Art Series
and
Dover Pictorial Archive Series
Dover Publications, Inc.
Mineola, New York

All other illustrations by Eileen Gerne Ciavarella

ISBN 0-87628-458-6 (S) ISBN 0-87628-459-4 (P)

ATTENTION: CORPORATIONS AND SCHOOLS

The Center for Applied Research in Education books are available at quantity
discounts with bulk purchase for educational, business, or sales promotional use. For
information, please write to: Prentice Hall Career & Personal Development Special
Sales, 240 Frisch Court, Paramus, New Jersey 07652. Please supply: title of book, ISBN
number, quantity, how the book will be used, date needed.

THE CENTER FOR APPLIED RESEARCH
IN EDUCATION
West Nyack, NY 10994
A Simon & Schuster Company

On the World Wide Web at http://www.phdirect.com

Prentice-Hall International (UK) Limited, *London*
Prentice-Hall of Australia Pty. Limited, *Sydney*
Prentice-Hall Canada Inc., *Toronto*
Prentice-Hall Hispanoamericana, S.A., *Mexico*
Prentice-Hall of India Private Limited, *New Delhi*
Prentice-Hall of Japan, Inc., *Tokyo*
Simon & Schuster Asia Pte. Ltd., *Singapore*
Editora Prentice-Hall do Brasil, Ltda., *Rio de Janeiro*

ABOUT THE AUTHOR

Judie Strouf is an experienced educator and author of materials for elementary and secondary teachers. Her teaching certificates and degrees are from Central Michigan University and Western Michigan University. In addition, she has taken advanced training at the University of Michigan and was the recipient of a Fulbright Scholarship from the United States Office of Education in Washington, D.C., to serve as an exchange teacher in England. She has traveled extensively, studying educational institutions and supervising student teachers both here and abroad.

Her major teaching and counseling experiences have been at Harper Creek Community Schools in Battle Creek, Michigan; Harbor Springs Community Schools in Harbor Springs, Michigan; and Chipping Norton Grammar School in Chipping Norton, England.

OTHER BOOKS
BY THIS AUTHOR

Hooked on Language Arts! Ready-to-Use Activities and Worksheets for Grades 4-8, The Center for Applied Research in Education, West Nyack, New York, 1990.

Americas Discovery Activities Kit: Ready-to-Use Worksheets for the Age of Exploration, The Center for Applied Research in Education, West Nyack, New York, 1991.

Hooked on the U.S.A.: Activities for Studying the States, J. Weston Walch, Portland, Maine, 1993.

The Literature Teacher's Book of Lists, The Center for Applied Research in Education, West Nyack, New York, 1993.

Primary Teacher's Book of Instant Word Games, The Center for Applied Research in Education, West Nyack, New York, 1996.

ABOUT THIS RESOURCE

This collection of 204 student-tested activities (individual puzzles, as well as group games) is based on the essential elements and competencies commonly taught in grades 4–6. It is a natural sequel to *Primary Teacher's Book of Instant Word Games,* designed for grades K–3.

To have real value, word games should be more than diversions, busy-work, or time-fillers. This collection is designed to be educationally sound and relevant to the upper elementary language arts/reading/spelling curriculum. In addition, 60 puzzle sheets help extend literacy in the content areas of social studies, science, mathematics, and the arts. An additional section provides fun while learning library skills.

The projects are practical whether you use a basal text or whole language approach. You can use these ideas to introduce a concept, add to regular lessons, follow-up after teaching, reward early finishers, or as sponge activities. Enjoyable, content-oriented challenges add spice to your classes and help students avoid the boredom that can result from the inevitable drill needed to develop and maintain skills at this age.

Puzzles originated with Egyptians and Romans many years ago; the best ones have endured. Thus, some of the games and puzzles herein are based on earlier sources and given new twists to serve an educational function for elementary students today. Other activities are fresh and original.

But why teach with games and puzzles?

Word games and puzzles deliver an added dimension to any curricula, but stimulating, fun activities are *essential* for upper elementary teachers. The clear and constant need for continued reteaching, reinforcement, and review throughout these crucial grades dictates that effective teachers incorporate supplementary, "lighter" non-textbook materials.

Other specific benefits of games and puzzles:

- Release tension and energy
- Challenge faster thinkers
- Enhance self concept
- Improve problem-solving skills
- Promote cooperative group behavior
- Develop positive feeling for language
- Turn extra or wasted time into productive learning
- Help relax and heal by evoking laughter
- Capture attention of reluctant learners
- Provide focus on particular skills or concepts
- Allow teacher OR student leadership
- Furnish change of pace and avert boredom
- Require minimal, if any, teacher preparation

A unique feature of *Intermediate Teacher's Book of Instant Word Games* is that, in addition to the usual word search, crossword, maze, and dot-connecting puzzles commonly found in elementary puzzle and game books, a wide range of OTHER techniques and devices are also employed. Proverb puzzles, cryptograms and codes, scrambled words and anagrams, roundabouts, word squares and circles, word ladders, word chains, secret messages, tic-tac-toes, team relays, guessing games, races, word pattern activities, word wheels, flash and response cards, alphabet games, riddles, puns, and other modes insure that your children won't ever say, "Not this again!" You will have something different and interesting to present each day of the school year.

The games focus on making all students "winners." Children win because they get practice in various skills and develop competencies needed for effective communication. Individual competition is down-played, while group, partnership, and team spirit is encouraged. As many students as possible are fully engaged during an activity, rather than being "losers," called "out," sitting down, or otherwise temporarily banished from the game. This important educational principle distinguishes this word game book from many other self-described "game books."

Activities are not labeled by grade levels because of the massive variance in abilities among students in single classrooms and among school curricula in different geographical areas. After minimal experimentation, you will find the instant games and puzzles that excite *your* students and most efficiently accomplish your goals. You will be gratified when students ask (or even coax and cajole) you to let them play certain games. Usually the simplest, easiest to play, and fastest-moving become their favorites. They are also very adept at making up their own puzzles and games, and should be encouraged to do so.

The TABLE OF CONTENTS provides a complete listing of appropriate, reproducible pages for the skills you want to reinforce, as well as separate listings of small- and large-group games. Don't miss the APPENDICES, which give hints on using games and puzzles with your students, instructions for making or using specific items, and other special teacher notes, referred to throughout the text in the upper right-hand corner of the pages as N-1 through N-24. Of course, a complete ANSWER KEY is included.

I hope this book creates enthusiasm and captures the cooperative and competitive spirits of your students. If they can learn and enjoy at the same time, *you* will be pleased, *they* will be pleased, and so will I!

Judie L. H. Strouf

CONTENTS

SECTION ONE:
VOCABULARY, SPELLING, AND WORD STRUCTURE—1

Individual Reproducibles

Contents

Group Games and Materials

SECTION TWO:
GRAMMAR, PUNCTUATION, AND WRITING—61

Individual Reproducibles

SECTION THREE:
READING AND LITERATURE—101

Contents

SECTION FOUR:
SOCIAL STUDIES, SCIENCE, MATHEMATICS, AND THE ARTS—143

SECTION FIVE:
LIBRARY AND REFERENCE—209

SECTION SIX:
HOLIDAYS AND SEASONS—237

APPENDIX ONE:
GENERIC AIDS—249

APPENDIX TWO:
TEACHER NOTES N-1 THROUGH N-24—259

APPENDIX THREE:
ANSWER KEY—265

Section One

VOCABULARY, SPELLING, AND WORD STRUCTURE

© 1996 by The Center for Applied Research in Education

1-1   SECRET WORD SCRAMBLE

Fill in the letters of the words that fit the definitions. Then find the secret word by <u>rearranging</u> the letters in the circles. Write the secret word in the circles at the bottom of the page.

1. A clothing fastener.

  —— —— ◯ —— —— ——

2. An early settler; the first of its kind.

  —— —— —— ◯ —— —— ——

3. A major road.

  —— —— —— —— —— ◯ ——

4. A heated discussion.

  —— —— —— ◯ —— —— —— ——

5. Something unexpected.

  ◯ —— —— —— —— —— —— ——

6. A safety and protection group.

  —— ◯ —— —— —— ——

7. The digesting area of the body.

  —— —— —— —— ◯ —— ——

8. A section of a book.

  —— —— —— —— ◯ —— ——

9. A nut-eating animal.

  —— —— —— —— ◯ —— —— ——

Secret Word Clue: Spaced out

Secret Word: ◯ ◯ ◯ ◯ ◯ ◯ ◯ ◯ ◯

1-2   DIAMOND IN THE ROUGH (MEDIUM)

See how many words you can form from the letters in this diamond. Each word must be four or more letters and use the middle letter of the diamond. The letters do not have to be touching each other. One word will use all the letters!

You cannot use any letter more than once. Proper nouns and contractions are outlawed. Each word counts a point, but you get five extra points if you figure out the nine-letter word. Do not use any word ending in s.

_____ _____ _____

_____ _____ _____

_____ _____ _____

_____ _____ _____

_____ _____ _____

_____ _____ _____

_____ _____ _____

_____ _____ _____

_____ _____ _____

_____ _____ _____

Clue to 9-letter word: Before kindergarten

Answer: ____ ____ ____ ____ ____ ____ ____ ____ ____

4

1-3 DIAMOND IN THE ROUGH (ADVANCED)

See how many words you can find using the letters in this diamond. Each word must be four or more letters and use the middle letter of the diamond. The letters do not have to be touching each other. One word will use all the letters!

You cannot use any letter more than once. Proper nouns and contractions are outlawed. Don't use words ending in <u>s</u> if you have already used a similar word form. Each word counts a point, but you get five extra points if you figure out the nine-letter word.

_____   _____   _____

_____   _____   _____

_____   _____   _____

_____   _____   _____

_____   _____   _____

_____   _____   _____

_____   _____   _____

_____   _____   _____

_____   _____   _____

_____   _____   _____

Clue to 9-letter word: Vanish

Answer: ____ ____ ____ ____ ____ ____ ____ ____ ____

1-4   ANIMAWHIRL

This is called an animawhirl because you whirl around and around to fill in names of animals. Fill in the animal names, using the numbers and clues to help you. The last letter of each animal will be the first letter of the next one.

Example: <u>cow</u>, <u>wolf</u>, <u>fox</u> would become <u>cowolfox</u> in the puzzle.

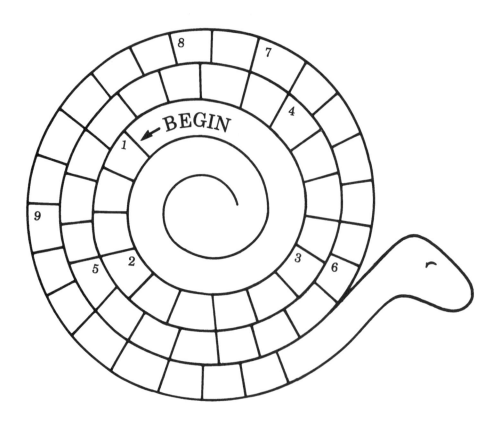

Clues:

1. Sometimes I'm a little grizzly.

2. I'm just a funny bunny.

3. I'm a big cat, so don't try to hold me by the tail.

4. I have a horn on my nose, but I don't toot it.

5. Sometimes I feel like a nut; sometimes I don't.

6. People say I can't change my spots.

7. Lassie and Rin-Tin-Tin are friends of mine.

8. Excuse my long neck, but I need it to eat leaves.

9. People say I never forget, but I sometimes do.

Name _____

1-5 VEGGIWHIRL

This is called a veggiwhirl because you whirl around and around to fill in names of vegetables. Fill in the vegetable names, using the numbers and clues to help you. The last letter of each vegetable will be the first letter of the next one.

Example: <u>cauliflower</u>, <u>radish</u> would become <u>caulifloweradish</u> in the puzzle.

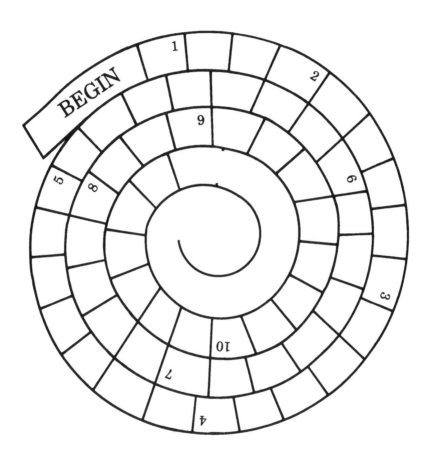

Clues:

1. Deep red; round
2. White; carrot-shaped
3. Green; bell-shaped
4. Yellow; carrot-shaped
5. Green; flower-like

6. Purple; egg-shaped
7. Bright red; round
8. Used in gumbo soup
9. Green stalks and tips
10. Popeye's favorite

Name _____

1-6   FORWARD AND REVERSE

Fill in the longest words you can think of that begin and end with the letters shown. Give yourself one point for each letter for use, including the letters given. Total your own points.

Example: W _____ S

You might think of WORDS for five points.

		POINTS
L _____ S		_____
E _____ R		_____
T _____ E		_____
T _____ T		_____
E _____ T		_____
R _____ E		_____
S _____ L		_____
	TOTAL	_____

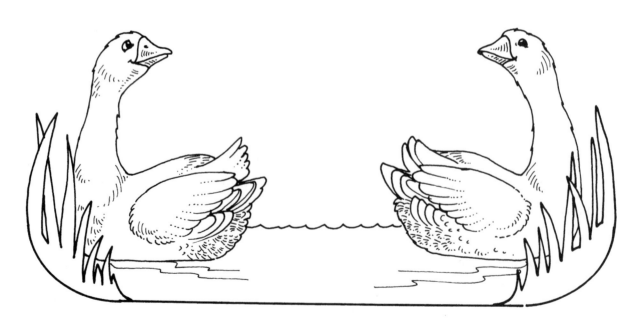

1-7   WORD PYRAMID

Fill in the word pyramid with words beginning and ending with the letters as shown. Use the definitions to help you.

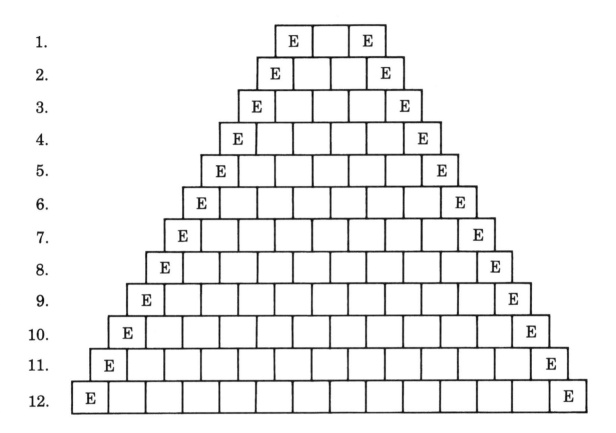

1.
2.
3.
4.
5.
6.
7.
8.
9.
10.
11.
12.

Definitions:

1. the evening before
2. side; border; margin
3. rub out
4. eatable
5. teach; instruct
6. legally qualified

7. exclude; remove
8. magnify; overstate
9. money spent
10. write opinions
11. prohibit church membership
12. capable of being put out

1-8   IDENTICAL FRONTS AND BACKS

These words have identical fronts and backs. See if you can figure them out using the clues.

1. O N ____ O N
2. S E ____ S E
3. M A ____ M A
4. E D ____ E D
5. S A ____ S A

6. T O ____ ____ T O
7. E R ____ ____ E R
8. O R ____ ____ O R
9. E M ____ ____ E M
10. R E ____ ____ R E

11. D E ____ ____ D E
12. D E ____ ____ D E
13. D E ____ ____ D E
14. D E ____ ____ D E
15. D E ____ ____ D E

Clues:

1. edible plant with strong odor
2. hearing is one example
3. liquid material under Earth's crust
4. bordered
5. hot, Mexican sauce
6. round, red vegetable
7. item used to rub out writing
8. formal speaker
9. symbol; badge
10. go to bed; stop working
11. translate a cryptic message
12. come to a decision
13. ten years
14. make fun of; scoff
15. cheat; trick

Add these missing <u>letters</u>: 9 + 7 + 10 + 2 + 3. _____

If you are right, your new word will mean <u>exploding with dynamite.</u>

1-9   THREE-LETTER WORD BLOCKS

Circle ONE letter from each pair in the box so that three 3-letter words are formed in both rows and columns. Write the six 3-letter words you created for each set below.

Set I

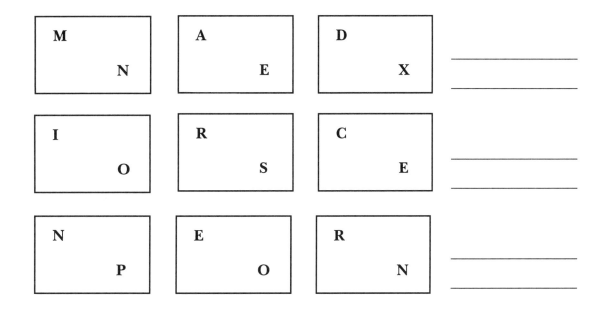

Set II

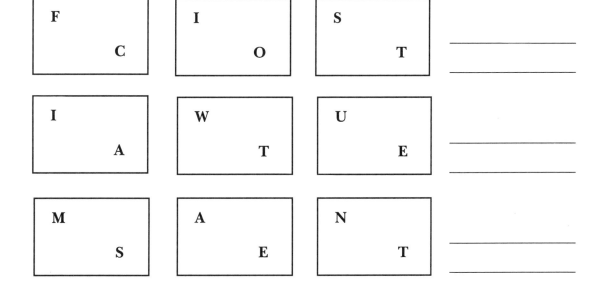

11

1-10   **FOUR-LETTER WORD BLOCKS**

Circle ONE letter from each pair in the box so that four 4-letter words are formed in both rows and columns. Write the eight 4-letter words you created below.

I
    B
	N
	    O
		O
		    T
			C
			    O

E
    R
	O
	    V
		M
		    A
			M
			    A

G
    O
	E
	    N
		C
		    R
			E
			    Y

N
    G
	E
	    X
		N
		    O
			N
			    A

_____

_____

_____

_____

_____

_____

© 1996 by The Center for Applied Research in Education

1-11   ANALOGIES

An analogy shows the relationship or likeness between things. For example, <u>bird</u> is to <u>fly</u> as <u>fish</u> is to <u>swim.</u> Fill out the blanks in the chart below to show the proper relationships.

This	is to this	as	this	is to this.
bird	fly		fish	1.
trunk	elephant		2.	pig
boy	man		girl	3.
4.	children		woman	women
sculptor	5.		artist	paint
subtract	remainder		add	6.
up	down		7.	out
happy	8.		joyful	blue
9.	numbers		English	words
duck	quack		10.	moo
chicken	11.		cat	paw
goose	gander		12.	doe
Christmas	tree		Halloween	13.
14.	under		black	white
more	less		even	15.
eye	16.		ear	hear
skin	person		17.	dog
18.	cry		sit	stand
baseball	home run		football	19.
six	twelve		20.	ten

1-12   CATS AND RATS

Some of these cats and rats are missing their heads; others are missing their tails. Fill in their missing parts.

1. CAT ____ ____   (opposite of throw)

2. CAT ____ ____ ____   (snooze)

3. CAT ____ ____ ____   (red sauce)

4. CAT ____ ____ ____ ____   (book or list of items)

5. CAT ____ ____ ____ ____ ____ ____   (church)

6. ____ CAT   ("Shoo! Go away!")

7. ____ ____ ____ CAT   (bay lynx)

8. ____ ____ ____ CAT   (male feline)

9. ____ ____ ____ ____ CAT   (one who imitates others)

10. ____ ____ ____ ____ CAT   (jungle feline)

11. RAT ____   (fee)

12. RAT ____ ____   (proportion)

13. RAT ____ ____ ____   (soldier's meal portion)

14. RAT ____ ____ ____   (shake)

15. RAT ____ ____ ____ ____ ____ ____ ____ ____   (poisonous reptile)

16. ____ RAT   (mean, unruly child)

17. ____ ____ RAT   (jewel weight)

18. ____ ____ ____ ____ RAT   (river animal)

19. ____ ____ ____ ____ ____ RAT   (opposite of Republican)

20. ____ ____ ____ ____ ____ ____ ____ RAT   (of highest social class)

1-13   GRAPH ROOTS (SET I)

Often many related words can be formed from the same root word and such is the case with <u>graph</u>. <u>Graph</u> means <u>something that writes or records.</u> Fill in as many as you can that have graph roots. Each space represents a missing letter.

Hint: The words are in alphabetical order to help you a bit.

1. ___ ___ ___ ___ GRAPH   (written name)

2. ___ ___ ___ ___ ___ ___ GRAPH   (recording heart)

3. ___ ___ ___ ___ ___ ___ GRAPH   (recording time)

4. ___ ___ ___ ___ ___ ___ GRAPH   (written in code)

5. ___ ___ ___ ___ ___ ___ ___ ___ ___ ___ ___ ___ GRAPH

                 (recording heart [as #2])

6. ___ ___ ___ GRAPH   (written tribute)

7. ___ ___ ___ ___ GRAPH   (all handwritten)

8. ___ ___ ___ ___ GRAPH   (run/run; [sock/baseball])

9. ___ ___ ___ ___ ___ GRAPH   (reprinting machine)

10. ___ ___ ___ ___ GRAPH   (written on subject)

11. ___ ___ ___ ___ GRAPH   (related sentences)

12. ___ ___ ___ ___ ___ GRAPH   (plays recorded music)

13. ___ ___ ___ ___ ___ GRAPH   (picture writing)

14. ___ ___ ___ ___ GRAPH   (recording lies)

15. ___ ___ ___ ___ ___ ___ GRAPH   (recording earthquakes)

16. ___ ___ ___ ___ GRAPH   (sending messages [wire])

15

Name _____

1-14   GRAPH ROOTS (SET II)

    Often many related words can be formed from the same root word and such is the case with <u>graph</u>. <u>Graph</u> means <u>something that writes or records.</u> Fill in as many words as you can that have graph roots. Each space represents a missing letter.
    Hint: The words are in alphabetical order to help you a bit.

1. ___ ___ ___ ___ ___ ___ ___ GRAPH ___   (life written by self)

2. ___ ___ ___ ___ ___ ___ GRAPH ___   (recording of sources)

3. ___ ___ ___ GRAPH ___   (life written by others)

4. ___ ___ ___ ___ ___ GRAPH ___   (handwriting as art)

5. ___ ___ ___ ___ ___ GRAPH ___   (recording places [maps])

6. ___ ___ ___ ___ ___ ___ GRAPH ___   (recording dance steps)

7. ___ ___ ___ ___ ___ ___ ___ ___ GRAPH ___
    (making motion pictures)

8. ___ ___ ___ ___ GRAPH ___   (recording statistics)

9. ___ ___ ___ GRAPH ___   (recording of places)

10. ___ ___ ___ ___ ___ ___ GRAPH ___   (writing dictionaries)

11. ___ ___ ___ ___ ___ GRAPH ___   (recording breast tissue)

12. ___ ___ ___ ___ ___ ___ GRAPH ___   (recording oceans)

13. ___ ___ ___ ___ ___ GRAPH ___   (taking pictures)

14. ___ ___ ___ ___ ___ GRAPH ___   (vile writing or pictures)

15. ___ ___ ___ ___ ___ GRAPH ___   (taking notes from speech)

16. ___ ___ ___ ___ GRAPH ___   (describing land or place)

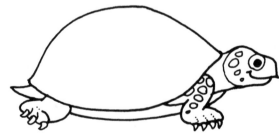

1-15   **ARTY WORDS**

All eighteen words have <u>art</u> in them, though only a few relate to art. Use the clues and see how many you can figure out. Write the missing letters on the blanks.

Words	**Clues**
1. ____ ART ____ ____	cardboard container
2. ____ ART ____ ____	top of automobile
3. ____ ART ____ ____	trade
4. ____ ART ____ ____	holds stockings (old fashioned)
5. ____ ART ____ ____ ____	opposite of nearer
6. ____ ART ____ ____ ____	member of a team of two
7. ____ ART ____ ____ ____	comic strip or movie
8. ____ ART ____ ____ ____	from Mars
9. ____ ____ ART ____ ____	office document to begin
10. ____ ____ ART ____ ____	four-person singing group
11. ____ ____ ART ____ ____	surprise
12. ____ ____ ART ____ ____	twenty-five cents
13. ART ____ ____ ____	person who draws or paints
14. ART ____ ____ ____	large vein
15. ART ____ ____ ____ ____	written newspaper piece
16. ART ____ ____ ____ ____ ____ ____	vegetable
17. ART ____ ____ ____ ____ ____ ____	disease involving stiffness
18. ART ____ ____ ____ ____ ____ ____ ____	not real

1-16   COMMON CENTS

These common words all contain <u>cent.</u> Sometimes the letters mean 100, but not always. See how many you can fill in.

1. 100 years   CENT ____ ____ ____

2. Fictitious creature:
    part man, part horse   CENT ____ ____ ____

3. The middle   CENT ____ ____

4. 100-year celebration   CENT ____ ____ ____ ____ ____ ____

5. Insect with many legs   CENT ____ ____ ____ ____ ____

6. A national or regional
    way of speaking   ____ ____ CENT

7. A way leading up; slope   ____ ____ CENT

8. Per hundred   ____ ____ ____ CENT

9. A short time ago   ____ ____ CENT

10. Odor   ____ CENT

On the lines below make up your own list of words containing <u>cent.</u> Some interesting words contain these letters in the middle, too!

_____   _____

_____   _____

_____   _____

_____   _____

_____   _____

Name _____

1-17   **VOCAB FUN**

Add or subtract one letter from the front or the back of the underlined word to form a new word that makes sense in the sentence. Put the new word in the box.

1. When a person has ⬜ , he can be a <u>danger</u> to others.

2. You must be quite ⬜ to be a good <u>climber.</u>

3. If you are a good ⬜ , you may be a good <u>earner.</u>

4. To catch some sun ⬜ we took our lunch <u>trays</u> outside.

5. It is sometimes ⬜ to get a great <u>deal</u> on a car.

6. We wanted certain ⬜ that our <u>roof</u> would not leak.

7. When she wanted to ⬜ , she did it with great <u>ease.</u>

8. Sometimes having a ⬜ can be kind of <u>scary.</u>

9. People will never ⬜ that a bear needs a <u>den.</u>

10. When the voters ⬜ a candidate, they often <u>elect</u> her.

11. Parents often grow ⬜ when kids have nothing to <u>wear.</u>

12. When books have a ⬜ , students often remember <u>them.</u>

Now write two of your own sentences using the same formula: Add or subtract a letter from the front or back of the word to form your new word. Circle your two words.

1. _____

_____

_____

2. _____

_____

_____

1-18 NAME THAT SPORT

All sports, games, and hobbies have their own jargon. Jargon includes words that are peculiar to the particular pastime, but are seldom used anywhere else. Using the clues, write what activity you would be engaged in on the blanks.

1. throwing a pot   _____

2. casting a fly   _____

3. booting a disc   _____

4. going into a huddle   _____

5. winning game/love   _____

6. going to the penalty box _____

7. leading a bird   _____

8. missing a wicket   _____

9. stealing a base   _____

10. dribbling a ball   _____

11. icing the puck   _____

12. slipping a stitch   _____

13. teeing up   _____

14. tickling the ivories   _____

15. betting to show   _____

1-19   FAMOUS ATHLETES

Find the last names of famous athletes going clockwise around the track. Fill in the names in the blanks provided. There are no extra letters. The names are NOT in order!

```
A I R R Y A N S H O E M A K E R G R I F F
L                                         I
B     1. Track and Field  _____   T
Y     2. Boxing           _____   H
E                                         —
L     3. Tennis           _____   J
D     4. Skating          _____   O
A                                         Y
R     5. Baseball         _____   N
B     6. Car Racing       _____   E
S                                         R
N     7. Football         _____   E
A     8. Hockey           _____   V
V                                         E
E     9. Golf             _____   R
Y     10. Horse Racing    _____   T
T                                         F
T     11. Swimming        _____   O
E                                         R
P A N A T N O M Y K Z T E R G N A M E R
```

1-20   THINK OF A NAME

Work with a partner and think of names that end in every letter of the alphabet. The hardest one is done for you. (Let's pretend someone was named after a country, in this case, because a name ending in q is a real toughie!)

1. _____**a**   14. _____**n**

2. _____**b**   15. _____**o**

3. _____**c**   16. _____**p**

4. _____**d**   17.   Ira**q**

5. _____**e**   18. _____**r**

6. _____**f**   19. _____**s**

7. _____**g**   20. _____**t**

8. _____**h**   21. _____**u**

9. _____**i**   22. _____**v**

10. _____**j**   23. _____**w**

11. _____**k**   24. _____**x**

12. _____**l**   25. _____**y**

13. _____**m**   26. _____**z**

1-21   GUESS WHO OR WHAT I AM

Follow the clues and guess who or what I am.

1. My first is in something that lives in the water;
   My second's in "Oreo," but not in slaughter.
   My third is in Regis, but not Kathie Lee;
   My fourth is in daughter and also daddy.
   I used to be President and now am a car,
   But on the golf course, I never did star.

   Who or what am I?_____

2. My first is in something that may coil and strike;
   My second and fifth are exactly alike.
   My third is in plume, but not in blame;
   My fourth is in knarly and also in name.
   I am so common, I should ring your bell,
   Even if some people think that I smell!

   Who or what am I?_____

3. My first is like me when I'm meaning myself;
   My second's in reef, but not in elf.
   My third is a vowel that rhymes with hay;
   My fourth is found in both neighbor and neigh.
   I am a country that's been in the news
   Because I have oil that some others might lose.

   Who or what am I?_____

4. My first is the same as a "veg" in a pod;
   My second's in node, but not in nod.
   My third is in apple and also in peach;
   My last rhymes with star and is found in reach.
   I am something that's good to eat;
   When I am ripe, I cannot be beat!

   Who or what am I?_____

5. My first is in baby and also baboon;
   My second and third are both found in moon.
   My last is found in kangaroo
   But definitely not in bugaboo.
   I can take you anywhere,
   But treat me kindly; I might tear!

   Who or what am I?_____

1-22   SYNONYM MATCH

Match the scrambled words in the left column with the synonyms or meanings in the middle column. The only problem is that some of the letters have been separated and scrambled. Ignore the spaces and have fun! Write the correct words in the third column.

Scrambled Words	Synonyms/Meanings	Unscrambled Words
1. sue mum	place for artifacts	_____
2. coin tune	keep going	_____
3. bird stu	bother	_____
4. rat sit	painter	_____
5. tom cash	digestive organ	_____
6. relace	breakfast food	_____
7. a nou start	space explorer	_____
8. sage lion	car fuel	_____
9. listen	quiet	_____
10. pet car	rug	_____

© 1996 by The Center for Applied Research in Education

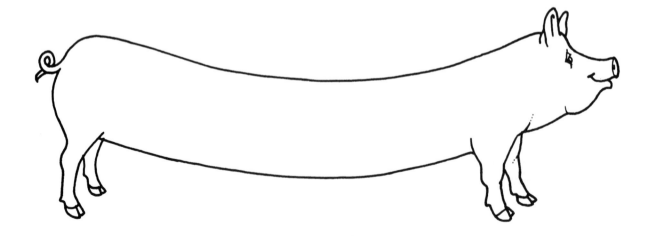

1-23   Tools of the Trade

The following are tools and other things you might find in a garage workshop. See how many you can identify. All the letters are there, but the workshop surely needs sorting out!

1. ridll   _____

2. was   _____

3. selchi   _____

4. diverrcrews   _____

5. sailn   _____

6. veell   _____

7. tib   _____

8. marhem   _____

9. sudswat   _____

10. borom   _____

© 1996 by The Center for Applied Research in Education

1-24   CONNOTATIONS AND DENOTATIONS

A connotation is a feeling or word that you think of when you hear a particular word. A denotation is the dictionary definition, synonym, or exact meaning of a word.

Example: SNAKE

    Denotation/Definition: reptile

    Possible Connotations: slimy; in the grass; poisonous; scaly; slithering

Look up any five nouns (names of things). Write the word on the first blank, a brief definition or synonym on the second blank, and your connotation on the third blank.

When everyone is finished, take turns reading either your dictionary definition or your connotation and have your classmates raise their hands if they think they know your word. Be sure to tell your classmates whether you are giving them the definition or connotation! Call on as many students as needed until your word is guessed. If they are having difficulty with the clue you gave them, try the opposite word (if you gave them the connotation, give them the definition or vice versa). The person who guesses correctly gets to say the next word to be guessed.

Word	Denotation/Synonym	Connotation
1. _____	_____	_____
	_____	_____
2. _____	_____	_____
	_____	_____
3. _____	_____	_____
	_____	_____
4. _____	_____	_____
	_____	_____
5. _____	_____	_____
	_____	_____

1-25 SPIDER SPELLING

See how many words you can form from this spider web. Follow the web in any direction, but do not go back over any letter of the web during the same word. Both singular and plural words count. No one-letter words count. Score yourself as follows:

2-letter words: 2 points
3-letter words: 3 points
4-letter words: 4 points
5-letter words: 5 points

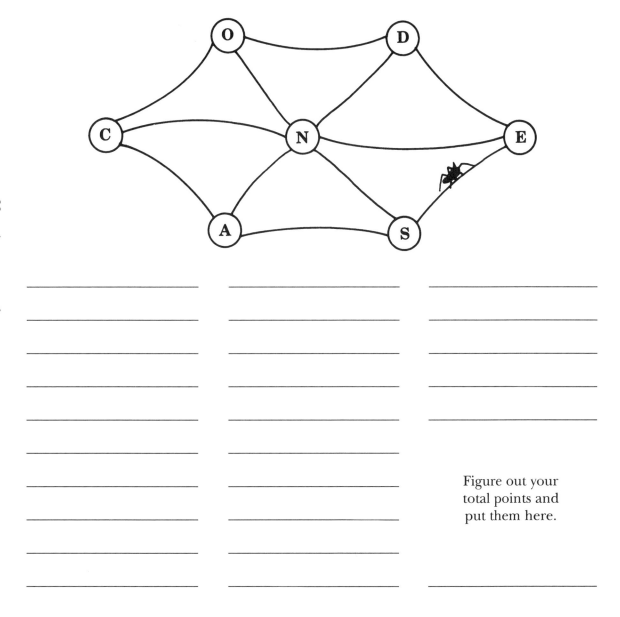

_____   _____   _____

_____   _____   _____

_____   _____   _____

_____   _____   _____

_____   _____   _____

_____   _____

_____   _____   Figure out your
                                                     total points and
_____   _____   put them here.

_____   _____

_____   _____   _____

1-26 THREE-LETTER WORD CIRCLES AND SQUARES

Take the twenty 3-letter words in the WORD BANK and fit them into the proper circles and squares. Each word will begin and end in a square. The words read from left to right and top to bottom. There is only one solution to the puzzle. You will have to use logic to eliminate the wrong possibilities. The corners of the large square are filled in to give you help in getting started.

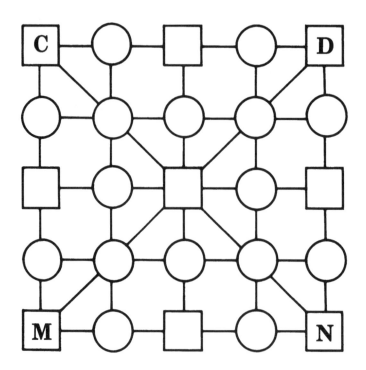

WORD BANK

CAN	GAP	NOR	RAT
CAR	GIN	NOT	TAM
COT	MAP	PIN	TAN
DOG	NOD	RAM	TAP
DOT	NOG	RAP	TUG

1-27   **THREE PLUS THREE**

Like Humpty Dumpty falling off the wall, these six-letter words from a fifth-grade spelling list got tumbled into parts. See if you can put their halves back together again.

SIL	LOC	GRO
WTH	MER	PLY
ATE	POL	CUE
SUP	RES	ENT
ITE	ARR	FAR
URE	FUT	IVE

1.

2.

3.

4.

5.

6.

7.

8.

9.

1-28   SPELLING DEMON MAZE

This is not a "made-up" list of spelling words. These words were taken directly from the writings of elementary students, and the misspellings are identical to the way the particular student spelled the words.

Follow the maze of misspelled words by shading in or coloring all incorrect words. On the lines below, write each word correctly.

address	layed	Febuary	fourty	where
all right	loveing	fierce	bouhgt	baloon
already	sevaral	height	poison	niether
although	swiming	tommorow	piece	coff **BEGIN**
chocolate	friend	wer'e	quit	half
color	untill	yow	wear	house
cough	gose	o'clock	weather	arithmetic

END

1. _____

2. _____

3. _____

4. _____

5. _____

6. _____

7. _____

8. _____

9. _____

10. _____

11. _____

12. _____

13. _____

14. _____

15. _____

© 1996 by The Center for Applied Research in Education

1-29   **WORD BUILDING**

The words in the WORD BUILDING BANK will fit into the three-letter column. The trick is to find out which one goes where. You will use the letters in the word (in the same order or rearranged) to form new words in each row using the letters given. You will build increasingly longer words as you go along. Good luck!

3 Letters	**4 Letters**	**5 Letters**	**6 Letters**	**7 Letters**
1. _ _ _	l _ _ _	r e _ _ _	M o n _ _ _	h o l i _ _ _
2. _ _ _	a _ _ _	p l _ _ _	_ _ _ r u n	h i d e _ _ _
3. _ _ _	_ _ a _	p a _ _ _	s m a _ _ _	c o u n _ _ _
4. _ _ _	n _ _ _	t r _ _ _	s t _ _ _ s	w _ _ l _ h y
5. _ _ _	_ _ _ e	s _ _ c _	_ _ c _ l e	_ _ _ c h e n

WORD BUILDING BANK

try   kit   day   out   tea

1-30   MYSTERY WORDS

Words are fun to play with. Use the clues to figure out the mystery words. Add them to the chart in the "Mystery Word" column. Then form a new word by adding the "Add-on Word" to the "Mystery Word." Put this new word in the last column.

Rhymes with	Backwards Means	Mystery Word	Add-On Word	New Word
1. jet	1/10 of 100		work	
2. ship	large hole		finger	
3. nut	bath place		ton	
4. snap	friend		land	
5. smile	placed		sun	
6. group	swim place		hole	
7. hum	cup		shoe	
8. chin	quick bite		hair	
9. spot	not bottom		tea	
10. school	stolen goods		box	

© 1996 by The Center for Applied Research in Education

1-31   <u>IE</u> OR <u>EI</u>

You have probably heard the following spelling rhyme:

<u>I</u> before <u>E</u>
Except after <u>C</u>
Or when sounded like <u>A</u>
As in neighbor or weigh.

     This means that <u>usually</u> <u>i</u> comes before <u>e</u> in a word with an <u>i-e</u> combination. When the combination comes right after <u>c</u>, you reverse it to <u>ei</u>. Also, when the combination sounds like <u>A</u>, you reverse it to <u>ei</u>. Use the rhyme as a guide to fill in the blanks.

1. rec____ve

2. retr____ve

3. bel____f

4. n____ghbor

5. ach____ve

6. al____n

7. dec____t

8. conc____ve

9. ch____f

10. ____ght

11. d____sel

12. qu____t

13. w____gh

14. b____ge

15. c____ling

16. p____ce

17. anx____ty

18. br____f

19. perc____ve

20. sl____gh

21. v____n

22. v____l

23. r____gn

24. r____n

25. p____r

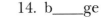

     To make matters more complicated, the following do NOT follow the rhyme. Knowing this, though, should make it easy for you! Just figure out what the rhyme would do, then do the opposite!

26. anc____nt

27. caff____ne

28. n____ther

29. counterf____t

30. ____ther

31. f____sty

32. forf____t

33. h____r

34. prot____n

35. s____ze

36. th____r

37. w____rd

1-32 **LETTER COMBOS**

Think of as many words as you can with the following letter combinations. The combos can appear anywhere in the word. Start with the first combo, think of as many as you can, then go on to the next. You can always go back later.

Scoring: words under 5 letters: 1 point each
words over 5 letters: 2 points each

ON

_____ _____ _____

_____ _____ _____

_____ _____ _____

_____ _____ _____

LE

_____ _____ _____

_____ _____ _____

_____ _____ _____

RT

_____ _____ _____

_____ _____ _____

_____ _____ _____

SE

_____ _____ _____

_____ _____ _____

_____ _____ _____

_____ _____ _____

1-33   WHAT DO WE HAVE IN COMMON?

Find the common letter in each set. Write the letters on the line and then unscramble to answer the question in the title.

1. famous
   homework
   lonesome
   matching
   wintertime

2. television
   officer
   phone
   accident
   recess

3. buffet
   campfire
   profit
   handkerchief
   suffix

4. opponent
   volunteer
   autograph
   geography
   speedometer

5. contract
   progress
   rebel
   clearance
   merchant

6. goodness
   understood
   introduce
   directly
   downward

7. shelf
   browse
   obtained
   loosely
   bulletin

SCRAMBLED WORD____ ____ ____ ____ ____ ____ ____

What do we have in common?

ANSWER:_____

© 1996 by The Center for Applied Research in Education

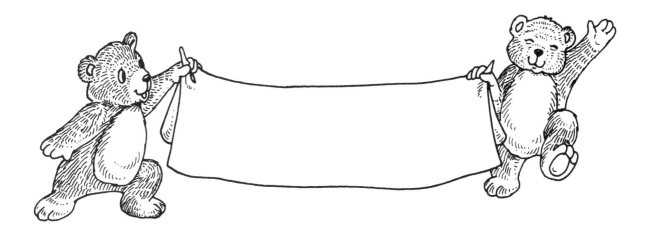

1-34   DROP AND ADD

Add or drop the first or last letter, one at a time, to form new words. Do not add either <u>s</u> or <u>d</u> at the <u>end</u> of a word. Use the lines to show the total number of letters needed.

1. s u p p e r

___ ___ ___ ___ ___

2. p a r e

___ ___ ___ ___ ___

3. f o r g e t

___ ___ ___ ___ ___

4. m o t h e r

___ ___ ___ ___ ___

5. t h i n g

___ ___ ___ ___

6. e v e

___ ___ ___

___ ___ ___ ___

7. b o a r d

___ ___ ___

___ ___ ___

8. l a t e r

___ ___ ___ ___

___ ___ ___

___

9. l a w

___ ___ ___ ___

10. s c o r e

___ ___ ___ ___

___ ___ ___

___ ___

11. f l a s h

___ ___ ___ ___

___ ___ ___

___ ___

___

12. l i c e

___ ___ ___ ___ ___

13. w o m e n

___ ___ ___ ___

___ ___ ___

___ ___

14. s w i t c h

___ ___ ___ ___ ___

___ ___ ___ ___

15. t h e i r

___ ___ ___ ___

1-35   ANAGRAM FILL-INS

Anagrams are words that use the same letters, but in different order. Each sentence below contains anagrams. The letters needed are in the ANAGRAM LETTERS BANK, but are scrambled. The anagrams in each sentence use the same letters. Each sentence uses a different set of letters to form words that fit.

1. The players made ☐ goals at the ☐ .

2. ☐ of the ☐ was to put a ☐ over the pit.

3. Put the ☐ on the ☐ before you ☐ by the ☐ office.

4. She sits in her ☐ , ☐ her cookies, and drinks her ☐ .

5. Their ☐ -felt goal was to save the ☐ .

6. The ☐ met their ☐ in the ☐ room.

7. The caveman ☐ his ☐ with his ☐ .

8. He shaved his ☐ , ☐ his chin, and ate ☐ .

9. The clerk's icy ☐ caused ☐ to flow as she heard about the high ☐ she would have to pay.

10. I will feel more ☐ ☐ , when I get some sleep.

ANAGRAM LETTERS BANK

abder   aelrt   aehrt   aerst   aeprs   aest   opst   ent   aprt   aemst

1-36   CONFOUNDING COMPOUNDS

Compound words are longer words formed from two or more separate words. See if you can combine the bricks from the brick pile to build a solid wall. Each brick contains a word that can be joined with another brick to form a compound word. The second brick of one compound word will be the first brick of the next.

Example:

air	mail	man

Hint: Use a pencil with a good eraser, because you will have several choices. Cross out words as you go. Make a solid wall!

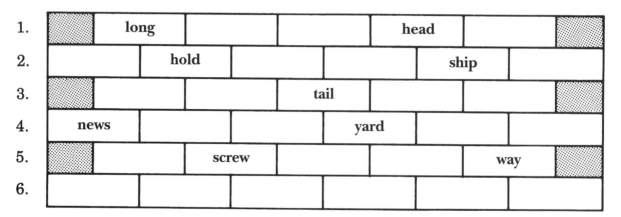

1. long | | | head | |
2. | hold | | | ship |
3. | | tail | | |
4. news | | yard | |
5. | screw | | | way |
6. | | | | |

Brick Pile:

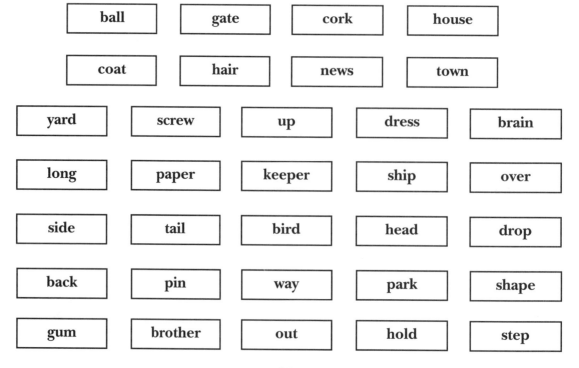

| ball | gate | cork | house |
| coat | hair | news | town |

yard	screw	up	dress	brain
long	paper	keeper	ship	over
side	tail	bird	head	drop
back	pin	way	park	shape
gum	brother	out	hold	step

© 1996 by The Center for Applied Research in Education

1-37   MIXED-UP MARTY (SET I)

Compound words are two separate words joined together to form a new word. Poor mixed-up Marty got the general idea, putting the correct parts at the beginnings, but paired the wrong parts for the endings! They <u>almost</u> make sense, but not quite. Match the parts correctly.

Hint: You may have a choice; use the MOST COMMON word, and you won't have any parts left over.

1. airdozer   _____

2. arrowmail   _____

3. barekeeper   _____

4. bullfly   _____

5. butterhead   _____

6. cowcake   _____

7. cupglass   _____

8. eggloaf   _____

9. eyeplant   _____

10. meatboy   _____

11. milkfall   _____

12. toadback   _____

13. watershake   _____

14. zoostool   _____

1-38   MIXED-UP MARTY (SET II)

Compound words are two separate words joined together to form a new word. Poor mixed-up Marty got the general idea, putting the correct parts at the beginnings, but paired the wrong parts for the endings! They <u>almost</u> make sense, but not quite. Match the parts correctly.

Hint: You may have a choice; use the MOST COMMON word, and you won't have any parts left over.

1. fishball   _____

2. footbox   _____

3. grasslife   _____

4. horsemower   _____

5. icehook   _____

6. jumphopper   _____

7. lawnshoe   _____

8. nighthorn   _____

9. quickrope   _____

10. quartersnake   _____

11. rattleback   _____

12. shoetoe   _____

13. tipfall   _____

14. wildsand   _____

1-?

FORWARD AND BACKWARD

b

v

...d words that form new words with other meanings when spelled
...; a list of several such words. Choose the best forward and back-
... the blanks. Remember, you will have to form the backward

began to <u>sag</u>; he was out of <u>gas</u>.

i

b.

bi

bo.

bud

bus

but

dew

got
gum
gut
lap
may
nap
net
nip
now
nub

pan
par
pat
pit
pot
rat
raw
saw
tam
ton

1. Yes, you _____ have a delicious _____ to eat.

2. Put your peppermint _____ in the _____ on the table.

3. Was it the regular school _____ or the _____?

4. The basketball hit the _____ _____ times.

5. Don't _____ the paint or you will have a _____ result.

6. What you _____ _____ a mirage.

7. _____ force is used in _____,.

8. The beady-eyed _____ got stuck in the black _____.

9. The _____ of the cooking _____ fit perfectly.

10. The coal did _____ quite weigh a _____.

11. _____ he knew the game was _____.

12. He wanted to use the shower, _____ had to use the _____.

13. My _____ put the papers in his _____.

Can you think of a sentence using one of the other forward-backward pairs? If so, put it on the line below.

_____

1-40   PREFIX FUN

A prefix consists of letters added to the beginning of a word that changes its meaning. Sometimes the new meanings relate to the root word; sometimes they don't seem to. In any case, it is fun to build new words this way. Add <u>pre</u> to words that match the definitions and build new words with the second meanings.

1. pre + (scrape)   = _____ (get ready)

2. pre + (walk slowly)   = _____ (start of document)

3. pre + (air opening)   = _____ (stop)

4. pre + (edge)   = _____ (conduct a meeting)

5. pre + (place)   = _____ (part of speech)

6. pre + (repair)   = _____ (beginning of word)

7. pre + (transmitted)   = _____ (gift)

8. pre + (speech)   = _____ (foretelling)

9. pre + (note-taker)   = _____ (recommend)

10. pre + (look after)   = _____ (fake)

11. pre + (countenance) = _____ (introduction)

12. pre + (give to)   = _____ (keep intact)

13. pre + (nervous)   = _____ (false action)

© 1996 by The Center for Applied Research in Education

1-41 SUFFIX FUN

Usually adding the suffix <u>er</u> makes a new word that relates to the root word. Here are a few where adding <u>er</u> has no relationship or the relationship is less obvious. Add <u>er</u> to words that match the definitions and build new words with the second meanings.

1. (performance)   +   er   =   _____ (light rain)

2. (cut)   +   er   =   _____ (lone gunner)

3. (caress)   +   er   =   _____ (larger)

4. (ship pole)   +   er   =   _____ (ruler; overlord)

5. (plus)   +   er   =   _____ (type of snake)

6. (back of boat)   +   er   =   _____ (later)

7. (snip)   +   er   =   _____ (prettier)

8. (haul behind)   +   er   =   _____ (tall spire)

9. (not lost)   +   er   =   _____ (originator)

10. (part of leg)   +   er   =   _____ (black eye)

11. (used in hockey)   +   er   =   _____ (purse lips)

12. (think through)   +   er   =   _____ (shop tool)

13. (container)   +   er   =   _____ (fighter)

14. (type of hat)   +   er   =   _____ (escapade)

15. (friend)   +   er   =   _____ (more ashen)

16. (vegetable)   +   er   =   _____ (right angle)

17. (cry loudly)   +   er   =   _____ (serious)

18. (kind of fish)   +   er   =   _____ (symbol worker)

19. (farm animal)   +   er   =   _____ (cringe in fear)

20. (in a line)   +   er   =   _____ (handles oars)

1-42   MISSING BRICKS: SUFFIXES

Fill in the bricks in the pyramid using the root words given and suffixes from the BRICKYARD. You will use some suffixes more than once. Use the following possibilities to help you:

(1)   Add suffix to root without any changes.

(2)   Drop e before adding suffix.

(3)   Double final consonant before adding suffix.

(4)   Change y to i before adding suffix.

penny		
critic		

run		
marry		
depend		
rate		
pretty		

happy			
attend			

```
                BRICKYARD

    ing          less          ize

    ed           ness          ent

    er           ant           ence

    est          ance
```

44

1-43   MISSING LINKS: SUFFIXES

Use the root words in the MISSING LINKS BANK to fill in all the missing links correctly. Where two words fit one suffix, you will have to choose the BEST link or you will end up with an extra word that won't fit.

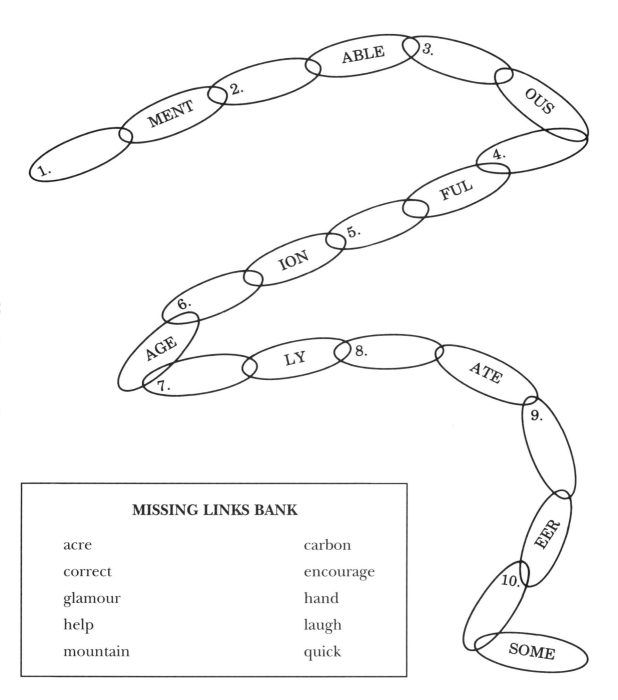

MISSING LINKS BANK

acre	carbon
correct	encourage
glamour	hand
help	laugh
mountain	quick

1-44   DROP DOWN AN AFFIX

Drop prefixes and suffixes from the boxes to the blanks below to form new words. You may use an affix more than once.

PREFIX BOX	AFFIX BOX
re	ment
under	ism
super	less
sub	tion
tri	ing
un	or
dis	ive
mid	ic
bi	ful

1. _____way

   _____way

   _____way

2. _____cycle

   _____cycle

   _____cycle

3. _____do

   _____do

4. _____charge

   _____charge

   _____charge

5. act_____

   act_____

   act_____

   act_____

6. harm_____

   harm_____

   harm_____

7. hero_____

   hero_____

8. attach_____

   attach_____

1-45 CONTRACTIONS DETECTIVE

Be a detective and find the letter or letters that have been left out to form the contractions (shortened forms) below.

After you finish, divide the circled letters into words and write the mystery message on the line provided.

Example: didn't = did not (the <u>o</u> has been left out to form the contraction).

1. aren't ____

2. can't ◯ ____ (add a letter!)

3. hadn't ____

4. hasn't ◯

5. haven't ____

6. he'll ◯ ____ (or) ◯ ____ ____

7. I'd ____ ____ ____ ____ (or) ◯ ____

8. I'll ____ ____ (or) ____ ____ ____

9. I've ____ ____

10. let's ____

11. she'd ____ ◯ ____ ____ (or) ____ ____

12. she'll ◯ ____ (or) ____ ____ ____ ____

13. they'd ____ ____ ◯ ____ (or) ____ ____

14. they'll ____ ____ (or) ◯ ◯ ____

15. weren't ◯

16. we'll ◯ ____ (or) ____ ____ ____

17. we've ____ ____

18. won't (substitutions used) ____ ____ ____ ____ (tricky one!)

19. you're ____

20. you've ____ ____

Write mystery message here: _____

1-46   REPEATERS

Many interesting words repeat their first syllables. Fill out the rest of the word from the clue given. Write the letter of the correct definition in front of each word. Then connect the letters of the definitions <u>in the order of your answers</u> to form a picture of another repeater word. Name the picture by filling out the repeater word on the blank given. (Dictionaries vary on spellings, so skip hyphens or spaces that may be appropriate in some of the words.)

Words

_____ 1. muu_____

_____ 2. tu_____

_____ 3. ma_____

_____ 4. pa_____

_____ 5. go_____

_____ 6. so_____

_____ 7. boo_____

_____ 8. bon_____

_____ 9. do_____

_____ 10. ho_____

Definitions

a. Santa's laugh

b. mistake (slang)

c. mother

d. Hawaiian dress

e. type of rock dancer

f. father

g. large, extinct bird

h. small piece of candy

i. fair to middling

j. ballerina's skirt

j ★   c ★

d ★   f ★
h ★   a ★

g ★

b ★   e ★

i ★

TOM_____

Name _____

1-47　　　　　PAIR O' WHAT?

The puzzle answers below all begin with <u>para.</u> Can you figure out what each pair represents? **Hint:** Watch spelling!

Example: more more = pair o' mores = paramours

1. _____　　　dice dice

2. _____　　　docks docks

3. _____　　　D D

4. _____　　　trooper trooper

5. _____　　　bull bull

6. _____　　　shoot shoot

7. _____　　　fin fin

8. _____　　　Keats Keats

9. _____　　　lies lies

10. _____　　　pet pet

11. _____　　　frays frays

12. _____　　　sight sight

13. _____　　　Saul Saul

14. _____　　　graph graph

1-48   HOMONYMS

Circle one letter in each pair of letters and make words across. The words in each set will be spelled differently, but pronounced the same (homonyms). Write the homonyms on the lines.

1. BR   OZ   TL   LT
   RB   OM   CL   ET

2. CL   OE   AN   NA
   LC   EO   AN   ET

3. SO   SO   AC   RT
   SO   SO   CR   TE

4. AV   AW   IQ   NO
   VA   WE   QI   ON

5. NF   LT   CA   RI   ER
   FN   TL   AC   RI   VR

6. CR   EX   AL   AL   EA   RO
   RS   EX   LA   LA   EA   RO

7. CZ   RO   MU   SR   RS   EA
   ZC   OR   AM   RS   SR   AE

8. BC   XA   PO   IJ   TB   IA   LF
   CB   AX   OP   JI   BT   IO   EL

9. EC   OF   UH   NK   CS   EA   LR
   EC   FO   HU   KN   SC   AI   LR

10. DP   RU   IC   NJ   CO   RI   PG   LA   AL
    PD   RU   CI   JN   CO   IR   GP   LE   EL

1. _____
   _____

2. _____
   _____

3. _____
   _____

4. _____
   _____

5. _____
   _____

6. _____
   _____

7. _____
   _____

8. _____
   _____

9. _____
   _____

10. _____
    _____

1-49   HOOKED-UP HOMONYMS

Homonyms can be words that are pronounced the same, but have different meanings and spellings. See how many homonyms you can hook together, yet make sense. To get you started, one word of the pair or trio is given. You can use it either at the beginning or the end of your hook-up. If you need to change tense by adding <u>ed</u> or <u>ing,</u> or add words, that's fair fare, but try for pared pairs.

Example: <u>sail</u> for <u>sale</u>

1. beat   _____

2. dual   _____

3. bear   _____

4. bawled   _____

5. band   _____

6. be   _____

7. beech   _____

8. burro   _____

9. sealing   _____

10. chilly   _____

11. doe   _____

12. patients   _____

13. mail   _____

14. hair   _____

15. night   _____

16. gnu   _____

17. flower   _____

18. ate   _____

19. horse   _____

20. peak   _____

1-50　　　HOMOPHONES

Add or subtract a letter from the front or back of each underlined word to form a homophone. Homophones are two words that sound alike.

1. The nurse was surprised to find a <u>nit</u> in the _____ cap.

2. The <u>lamb</u> seemed to be on the _____ as it scampered quickly away from the shepherd.

3. The students wondered if they could use _____ in a formula to figure the circumference of the <u>pie.</u>

4. The lawyer asked the jury to <u>please</u> hear her _____.

5. The baby sitter had to clean the <u>jam</u> from the door _____ before the baby's parents came home.

6. The furniture <u>in</u> the _____ were all antiques.

7. The couple was visiting a beautiful <u>isle</u> when they decided to march down the wedding _____ as soon as possible.

8. The paper <u>route</u> made it necessary to _____ several stray dogs from the area.

9. The shop students had to <u>wrack</u> their brains to figure out how to assemble the hat _____.

10. By the time the <u>bell</u> rang, the southern _____ knew she would be done with her homework.

11. The students had to <u>canvass</u> all the _____ shops to find just the right color for their project.

12. The <u>teas</u> were very formal, but there was no reason to _____ the hostess about it.

13. The <u>rest</u> of the by-standers had to _____ the gun from the robber's hand.

1-51   HOMOGRAPHS

The following homographs are spelled the same, but have different meanings and pronunciations. Use each word twice to fill in the correct blanks.

---

axes   bass   bow   buffet   commune   console   content   converse
desert   does   dove   entrance   intimate   live   minute
present   refuse   row   wind

_____ 1. happy

_____ 2. leave

_____ 3. give sympathy

_____ 4. fish

_____ 5. female deer (*pl.*)

_____ 6. have life

_____ 7. strike

_____ 8. 60 seconds

_____ 9. live together

_____ 10. give

_____ 11. talk

_____ 12. trash

_____ 13. line

_____ 14. axis (*pl.*)

_____ 15. turn

_____ 16. bird

_____ 17. opening

_____ 18. gift

_____ 19. things inside

_____ 20. dive (*past tense*)

_____ 21. tools

_____ 22. opposite

_____ 23. tied ribbon

_____ 24. charm

_____ 25. cabinet

_____ 26. personal

_____ 27. suggest

_____ 28. low voice

_____ 29. arid area

_____ 30. exist

_____ 31. meal

_____ 32. tiny

_____ 33. say no

_____ 34. get in touch with

_____ 35. fight

_____ 36. bend

_____ 37. air current

_____ 38. part of "to do"

1-52   PALINDROMES

A palindrome is a word or phrase that is spelled the same both forward and backward. With this knowledge fill in the missing letters in the puzzle to form words that are palindromes.

1. | S | O | L | | |

2. | | | Y | A | K |

3. | S | T | A | | |

4. | M | | D | A | |

5. | R | A | | A | R |

6. | | | G | A | S |

7. | S | | A | H | |

8. | L | | V | | L |

9. | | I | V | I | |

10. | R | E | | | |

11. | | | | D | E | |

Name _____

1-53   **PALINDROME CHALLENGE**

A palindrome is a word or phrase spelled the same backward or forward. See if you can figure out these palindromes from the clues given.

1. [R] [ ] [ ] [I] [ ] [E] [ ]   _____

2. [ ] [E] [ ] [A] [ ] [ ] [R]   _____

3. [ ] [E] [ ] [F] [I] [ ] [ ]   _____

4. [R] [O] [T] [ ] [ ] [ ] [ ]   _____

5. [ ] [ ] [ ] [E] [T]   _____

6. [D] [ ] [ ] [ ]   _____

7. [M] [ ] [ ] [ ] [ ] , [ ] ['M] [A] [ ] [A] [ ]

_____

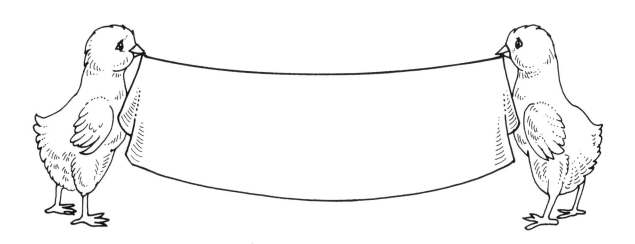

55

1-54   ACRONYMS: MADD MIA

An acronym is a group of catchy letters standing for words, often names of organizations. For example, SADD stands for Students Against Drunk Driving.

Enjoy the short paragraph about Mia. Write the meanings of the numbered acronyms on the lines provided below. PUSH* yourself. See if you can do it without AIDS.**

    (1)   (2)   (3)   (4)   (5)
MIA was MADD. She SAT on a WASP. It felt like a PIN. "Next
               (6)   (7)
time," she said, "I'll SWAT or MASH it! In the meantime, I'm going
  (8)   (9)   (10)
to PAC my bags, have a COLA, and GATT to the hospital. I need some
(11) (12)
CARE NOW."

1. _____

2. _____

3. _____

4. _____

5. _____

6. _____

7. _____

8. _____

9. _____

10. _____

11. _____

12. _____

* People United to Save Humanity

** Acquired Immune Deficiency Syndrome

© 1996 by The Center for Applied Research in Education

1-55   T 4 2

Some letters, letter combinations, or numbers sound like complete WORDS. For instance, the title of this word game sounds like "Tea for Two."

Here are some other fun letters and numbers. Write out what the two examples say. Then, on another sheet of paper, make up your own sentences using the letters and numbers in the list. Exchange your paper with a partner and figure out each other's sentences. If you need to use any <u>real</u> words, put them in parentheses (as shown in the first example).

Examples:

1. ICU (have) 2II. _____

2. O, RT, ILOU. _____

Single Letters

B	=	bee; be
C	=	sea; see
G	=	gee
I	=	I; eye
J	=	jay
K	=	Kay
O	=	owe; oh
R	=	are
T	=	tea
U	=	you; ewe
Y	=	why

Double Letters

BD	=	beady
CD	=	seedy
CU	=	see you
II	=	aye aye
IL	=	I'll; aisle; isle
IM	=	I'm
IO	=	I owe
IV	=	ivy
LN	=	Ellen
MT	=	empty
NV	=	envy
OP	=	Opie
PT	=	Petey
QT	=	cutie
RT	=	Arty
RU	=	are you
SA	=	essay
TP	=	tepee
VU	=	view

Triples are even more fun!

NME = enemy
NRG = energy

Add numbers or letter-number combinations for variety.

1	=	one; won
2	=	two; to; too
4	=	four; for
8	=	eight; ate
4T	=	forty; for tea
8T	=	eighty; ate tea

For plurals or other variations, use two of the same letters. Put a line over the top to show they go together.

$\overline{BB}$	=	bees
$\overline{CC}$	=	seas
$\overline{EE}$	=	ease
$\overline{II}$	=	eyes; ayes
$\overline{JJ}$	=	jays
$\overline{LL}$	=	else
$\overline{NN}$	=	ends
$\overline{OO}$	=	oh's
$\overline{QQ}$	=	cues
$\overline{TT}$	=	tease
$\overline{UU}$	=	use
$\overline{YY}$	=	wise

1-56   **ANAGRAM STEPS**

Anagrams are words that can be formed by arranging letters in a new way. See how far you can travel up the steps by adding a letter each step and rearranging the letters to form a new word. Remember, you MUST rearrange the letters each time!

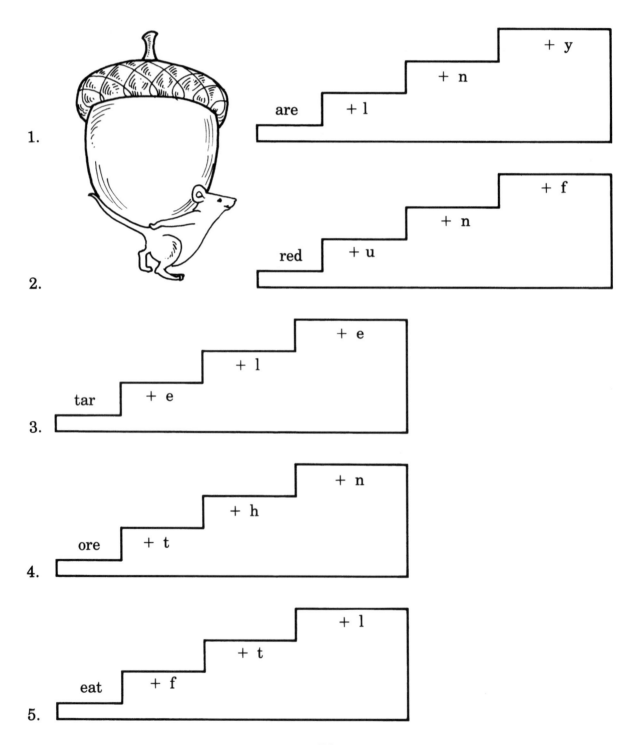

1.

are   + l   + n   + y

2.

red   + u   + n   + f

3.

tar   + e   + l   + e

4.

ore   + t   + h   + n

5.

eat   + f   + t   + l

1-57   PLURAL TIC-TAC-TOE

Play tic-tac-toe with a partner. Your goal is to win the game with a straight line (up, down, across, or diagonal) that includes ONLY PLURAL NOUNS. If you get really good at it, try playing reverse tic-tac-toe, with the <u>loser</u> being the one forced to make his or her straight line first!

OXEN	FOX	DEER
PIANOS	WOMEN	DOWNSTAIRS
ADDRESS	MISS	TEETH

How to Play Plural Tic-Tac-Toe:

1. Two people take turns marking squares on one sheet.

2. Each player tries to pick a square with a plural word in it.

3. Alternating turns, each player marks a square with a giant "X."

4. Each player tries to get three PLURAL words forming a straight line in any direction.

5. The player who first gets the correct tic-tac-toe (straight line) wins.

Hints:

1. Plural means more than one.

2. There is only one correct tic-tac-toe solution.

Modification: When you know these plurals well, each player can make up your own puzzle with words YOU choose. Be sure there is only one correct solution. Play several of your created games.

1-58   WORD SQUARES

Get into small groups. Each group member has a word square. Each player names a letter, which all members write on the line provided. Repeated letters are allowed. Avoid less common letters like q, z, and x, or you'll really make it hard on yourselves.

When everyone has the letters written down, fill in your word squares. Arrange the letters with as many 4- and 5-letter words as possible. Letters must form words horizontally and vertically (across and up and down). You may "black out" a letter square if not needed, but this is likely to reduce your total score.

See who can get the most points in your group, using the following point rewards:

1/2/3-letter words	=	0 points
4-letter words	=	5 points
5-letter words	=	10 points

Put the chosen letters of the alphabet on the line above. Use ONLY these letters to form your word square below.

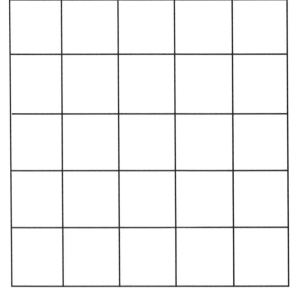

Score: Number of 4-letter words _____ × 5 = _____ (a)

Number of 5-letter words _____ × 10 = _____ (b)

Add a + b for Total Score _____

Section Two

GRAMMAR, PUNCTUATION, AND WRITING

Name _____

2-1   CHANGING NOUNS WITH S

Put an <u>s</u> in front of the correct word from the NOUN BANK to form a new word for each clue.

1. ___ ___ ___ ___ ___   football and basketball, for instance

2. ___ ___ ___ ___   ribbon worn as a belt

3. ___ ___ ___ ___   what you wear on one foot

4. ___ ___ ___ ___   cleaners might get this out

5. ___ ___ ___ ___   dirt

6. ___ ___ ___ ___   wound

7. ___ ___ ___ ___ ___ ___   turns something on and off

8. ___ ___ ___ ___   found in the kitchen

9. ___ ___ ___ ___ ___   tells which team is ahead

10. ___ ___ ___ ___ ___   odor

NOUN BANK			
core	port	pot	ore
hoe	ash	cent	
ink	witch	oil	

2-2 NOUNS: PEOPLE AND THINGS

These words are all nouns listed on "essential vocabulary" lists. See if you can classify them into people or things. Put a P in front of people; put a T in front of things.

Hint: Consider a noun like fireman "people," rather than a thing.

____adult	____flame	____police
____air	____fumes	____post office
____bus	____gasoline	____principal
____checkbook	____gate	____property
____crowd	____gentlemen	____safety
____dentist	____grass	____shelter
____doctor	____hands	____station
____door	____heat	____taxi
____dynamite	____ice	____teacher
____elevator	____instruction	____time
____entrance	____ladies	____tunnel
____exit	____nurse	____violator
____explosive	____pedestrian	____waiter
____fire escape	____poison	____water

Count the number of T's and put your answer here. _____

Count the number of P's and put your answer here. _____

Subtract (T's minus P's) and put your answer here. _____

If your final answer equals 8 + 8, you are probably correct.

2-3 NOUN/VERB SEARCH

Some words are nouns AND verbs. Circle any words going forward, backward, up, down, or diagonally that can be used both as nouns and verbs. Write the words below. There are at least 18.

P	T	A	L	K	E	F	B	I	J
L	R	B	E	N	D	A	N	C	E
A	A	E	C	M	R	X	H	L	N
Y	C	K	S	K	I	N	J	E	O
A	H	O	D	S	U	T	U	A	B
B	E	J	D	R	E	A	M	R	L
B	M	I	L	C	P	A	P	E	R

_____   _____   _____

_____   _____   _____

_____   _____   _____

_____   _____   _____

_____   _____   _____

2-4 BE PUNNY WITH ADJECTIVES AND NOUNS

A pun is a play on words. In the title above "punny" is a play on the word "funny." See if you can find <u>rhyming</u> puns that fit the following definitions.

Hint: There will be an adjective (describing word) and then a noun in each 2-word pun. Blanks indicate number of letters needed. The first one is done for you.

1. A rain-soaked cat   wet pet

2. A weak man   _ _ _ _ _   _ _ _ _

3. An escaped animal   _ _ _ _ _   _ _ _ _ _

4. A nasty, green vegetable   _ _ _ _   _ _ _ _

5. A street frog   _ _ _ _   _ _ _ _

6. An off-limits seashore   _ _ _ _ _   _ _ _ _ _

7. A sun-bathing male   _ _ _ _   _ _ _ _

8. A lady goose's dandruff   _ _ _ _ _ _   _ _ _ _ _ _ _

9. A resentful baby-tender   _ _ _ _ _ _   _ _ _ _ _ _

10. Sick girlfriend of Jack   _ _ _ _   _ _ _ _

11. A healthy, intelligent person   _ _ _ _ _ _   _ _ _ _ _ _ _

12. A chicken enclosure   _ _ _   _ _ _

13. A prison story   _ _ _ _ _   _ _ _ _ _

14. An unusual couple   _ _ _ _ _   _ _ _ _

15. A scalding pan   _ _ _   _ _ _

16. An obese Siamese   _ _ _   _ _ _ _

17. A fortunate baby fowl   _ _ _ _ _   _ _ _ _ _

18. An unambitious flower   _ _ _ _   _ _ _ _ _

19. A pale red wash basin   _ _ _ _   _ _ _ _

20. A very tiny hot dog   _ _ _ _ _   _ _ _ _ _ _

If you can, create a definition and rhyming pun of your own on the line below.

_____

2-5   ADJECTIVES THAT DESCRIBE ME

Put one letter of your first name on each short line. If your first name is shorter than five letters, add letters from your last name. Then look at the list of adjectives and pick out those that begin with the same letters as your name. Put them beside each letter. If you can't find a suitable adjective, you may add another.

1. _____   _____

2. _____   _____

3. _____   _____

4. _____   _____

5. _____   _____

active	gentle	mathematical	strong
aggressive	giving	mature	tender
beautiful	grand	noisy	terrific
bossy	happy	normal	tough
brave	helpful	odd	unafraid
calm	helpless	orderly	useful
careless	intelligent	organized	useless
cheerful	irrational	playful	vague
demanding	irritable	pleasant	vain
dependent	jealous	proud	warm
dreamy	jolly	quarrelsome	whiney
eager	jumpy	quiet	x-rated
emotional	kind	reasonable	x'd out
energetic	kooky	relaxed	yappy
fantastic	lazy	religious	young
friendly	lonely	shy	zealous
funny	mad	silly	zesty

2-6   BLEEPING THE ADJECTIVES

Write a short story or paragraph, but bleep out the adjectives (describing words). Write the word <u>bleep</u> wherever an adjective should go. At the bottom of the page, list the adjectives YOU would use.

Read your bleeped story to the class. Let them write down an adjective on the back of their paper every time you say <u>bleep.</u> Then choose someone else to read your story from your paper. That person hesitates and points to someone different every time there is a bleeped word. The person pointed to says the word he or she has written down for that spot, and the reader continues.

At the end, you reread your story as you wrote it, filling in the adjectives YOU used from your own paper. How much difference was there?

_____

_____

_____

_____

_____

_____

_____

_____

_____

_____

Adjectives:

1. _____   6. _____   11. _____

2. _____   7. _____   12. _____

3. _____   8. _____   13. _____

4. _____   9. _____   14. _____

5. _____   10. _____   15. _____

2-7   A CAN OF WORDS

Draw three words from the can and fill in the chart.

1. Put the words in alphabetical order in Column 1.

2. Tell what part of speech each word usually is in Column 2.

3. Tell how many syllables each word has in Column 3.

4. Write the vowels in each word in Column 4.

5. Write the consonants in each word in Column 5.

6. Use the words in a sentence on the lines below. (You may add words of your own, but be sure to use all three of the words you drew.)

	Column 1 WORDS	**Column 2** PARTS OF SPEECH	**Column 3** SYLLABLES	**Column 4** VOWELS	**Column 5** CONSONANTS
1.					
2.					
3.					

Sentence Using All Three Words:

_____

_____

_____

_____

_____

2-8   **PERSONALIZED SENTENCES**

Take the first five letters of your name and make a sentence using the letters to form the words in order. If your first name is shorter than five letters, borrow letters from your last name. If your first name is longer than five letters, drop off the rest.

Example: Name is Rosemary. First five letters (r o s e m).

Sample sentence: Rest or sleep ever more.

_____

_____

_____

Now take the first five letters of someone else's name in the room and follow the same directions as above.

_____

_____

_____

Variation: If you get good at this, try using your ENTIRE name, first and last.

_____

_____

_____

_____

_____

_____

2-9   DIVIDE AND CONQUER

Figure out the words that form the sentences below and write the sentences on the lines provided. Words in each sentence are divided improperly, but are in the correct order. If you divide them correctly, you will conquer the truth.

Example: C anyo ufig ureo utt hisen ten ce?

Answer: Can you figure out this sentence?

1. An ouni sthen am eofap ers on, pla ce, orth ing.

   _____.

2. Ad jecti vesde scri ben oun sand pron ouns.

   _____.

3. Pron ounsc anb epos sessi ve.

   _____.

4. Aglos sar yisl ike amin iat ured icti on ary.

   _____.

5. Ind exe sar eus uall yint heb acks ofbo oks.

   _____.

6. Yo uus eac ard cat al ogt ofin dab ook.

   _____.

7. Ane ncyc lop edi aisa goo dre fere nce.

   _____.

8. Wor dsca nbed ivid edin tos yllab les.

   _____.

2-10   SENTENCE A-MAZE-MENT

Follow the mazes (1, 2, 3, and 4). Put the best sentences you find on the correct lines below. You must use each word in order, not skip any words, and use all words provided. Be sure to include the correct capitalization and end punctuation.

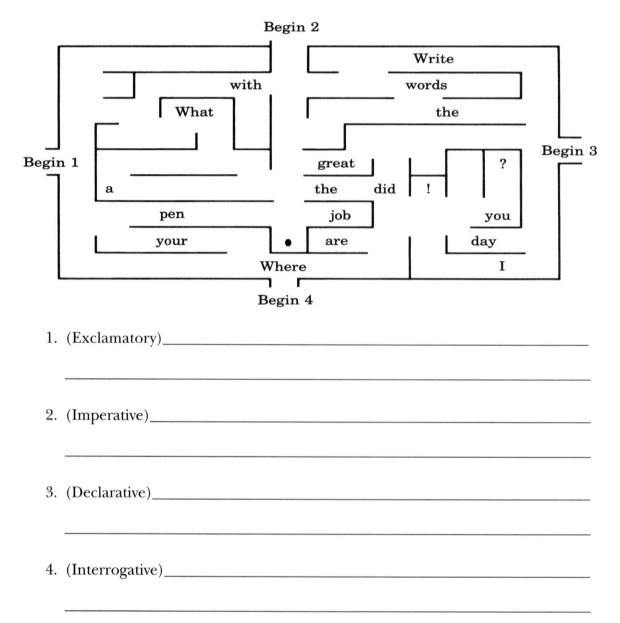

1. (Exclamatory)_____

_____

2. (Imperative)_____

_____

3. (Declarative)_____

_____

4. (Interrogative)_____

_____

Hints:

- An exclamatory sentence shows emotion and ends with an exclamation point.
- An imperative sentence commands or makes a request and ends with a period.
- A declarative sentence makes a statement and ends with a period.
- An interrogative sentence asks a question and ends with a question mark.

2-11   DO THESE SENTENCES RING A BELL?

Choose the correct letter from each pair of answers, and put it on the blank provided. Your goals are to recognize sentence fragments, run-on sentences, simple, compound, and complex sentences.

On the grid of dots, draw lines to connect the dots above the letter of each answer you gave. Do these sentences ring a bell?

1. _____ Are you going out for basketball this year?
       (a) simple (b) compound

2. _____ Marty had to serve in Desert Storm, but Jim didn't.
       (c) compound (d) complex

3. _____ Whenever we all got together for a family picnic.
       (e) simple (f) fragment

4. _____ Brandon is my best friend, he also is a good student.
       (g) simple (h) run-on

5. _____ When school is out, I plan to go straight home.
       (i) simple (j) complex

6. _____ After the football game in the back of the stadium.
       (k) fragment (l) compound

7. _____ All the people gathering together in a major huddle.
       (m) complex (n) fragment

8. _____ Stop it!
       (o) fragment (p) simple

9. _____ Artie and Sam saw a light, we were sure we could make it.
       (q) run-on (r) compound

10. _____ Give me a break, I didn't mean it.
       (s) complex (t) run-on

11. _____ Hilary didn't think so, but we really cared.
       (u) compound (v) simple

12. _____ Biding our time, waiting for the rain to stop falling.
       (w) run-on (x) fragment

13. _____ Shawn and Chris gave her the break that she needed.
       (y) complex (z) compound

73

2-12   Initial Sound Sentences

Make up a sentence (silly or not) from each of the following four-letter words. **Rules:** You must use a different classmate's name in each sentence. The words in your sentence must begin with the letters in the same order as the given words.

Example: POTS   <u>P</u>eter <u>o</u>ught <u>t</u>o <u>s</u>have.

1. SEND   _____

_____

2. JELL   _____

_____

3. HUNT   _____

_____

4. CLUB   _____

_____

5. SINK   _____

_____

6. FIRE   _____

_____

7. WAVE   _____

_____

8. LATE   _____

_____

9. DONE   _____

_____

10. GAME   _____

_____

2-13   **ALPHABET STORY**

Write a 26-word story with each word beginning with the next letter of the alphabet. Here is the alphabet to remind you of the sequence of letters and an example of how to do it.

A B C D E F G H I J K L M N O P Q R S T U V W X Y Z

Alphabet Story Example: Archie began coming down. Every friend gave him ideas. Just Kim lacked meaningful news. Others, perhaps quite reluctantly, shared their unassuming views. We xeroxed youthful zaniness.

_____

_____

_____

_____

_____

_____

_____

_____

Easier Version: Make up an alphabet story as above, but do not use the last four letters of the alphabet.

_____

_____

_____

_____

_____

2-14   LIVING STORY

Fill in the blanks with the names of trees or flowers to make a reasonably sensible story. Use the WORD GARDEN to help you.

(1)_____ and (2)_____ _____

were (3)_____ students. They made quite a (4)_____.

He often (5)_____ for a (6)_____, but her

(7)_____ objected and (8)_____ up against

(9)_____ _____. That made poor

(10)_____ (11)_____ a lot and

(12)_____. She thought she had old (13)_____

_____ in the (14)_____ of her hand, and didn't give

a (15)_____ about what he thought.

One day at (16)_____ _____,

(17)_____ decided to (18)_____ up in her best

bathing suit and go to the (19)_____. By (20)_____!

There was (21)_____ _____! He kissed her on her

(22)_____ and said, "You're the (23)_____ of my

eye. Will (24)_____ marry me?"

"Yes," she drawled. "I'll stay beside you as long as (25)_____."

WORD GARDEN

olive   spruce   palm   pear   yew   Sweet William   aster

gum   date   fig   Paw Paw   beech   poplar   balsam   Poppy

apple   tulips   Daisy   four o'clock   pine   rose

Hint: Daisy and Sweet William are used more than once.

© 1996 by The Center for Applied Research in Education

2-15 MISSING-LETTER STORY

Write a brief story or short paragraph on the lines below. Leave out ONE letter from the entire story. Don't misspell words; just use words that avoid that particular letter. Be careful to use all other letters in the alphabet somewhere in the story. Pass your story to classmates when you are done to see if they can figure out the missing letter.

Here is an example of a sentence that uses all the letters but one. Cross out the letters in alphabetical order. What letter is missing?

The quick brown fox jumped over the lazy dog.

MISSING LETTER: _____

_____

_____

_____

_____

_____

_____

_____

_____

_____

_____

_____

_____

_____

_____

2-16   PROOFREADING CHALLENGES

UNUSUAL PARAGRAPH

This paragraph is puzzling. It is a good paragraph, but it is missing what many paragraphs contain. It looks ordinary, and you wouldn't think anything was wrong with it at first, but if you look sharp, you will find out what it is. Study it hard. Can you find out quickly why this paragraph is so uncommon? Study it again. Think about it. Mull it around. Who knows? You may crack this nut and pick out a solution. Good luck!

Put your answer here: _____

WHY DON'T I LIKE THOSE THINGS?

Things I Like

coffee
dogs
cigars
nieces
nephews
movies
piano
chair
cola
milk

Things I Don't Like

tea
cats
cigarettes
brothers
sisters
television
letters
table
water
root beer

Put your answer here: _____

THE CASE OF THE MISSING LETTERS

These tongue-twisters are hard to read with or without their missing letters. Figure out a different missing letter in each one. Then try to say them three times very quickly!

R U E R A Y U G G Y U M P E R S

Put your answer here: _____

_____

E T E R I E R I C K E D A E C K O F I C K L E D E E R S

Put your answer here: _____

_____

2-17   # LETTER PARTS PUZZLE

The basic parts of a written letter are found in the LETTER PARTS BANK. Put them in the correct places in the puzzle.

© 1996 by The Center for Applied Research in Education

Across

3. written name

5. ending

Down

1. greeting

2. address and date

4. main part

LETTER PARTS BANK

closing   heading   salutation   signature   body

2-18   USE YOUR IMAGINATION AND PRACTICE PUNCTUATION

Below are examples of "What did one _____ say to the other _____?" The first few are completed. Use your imagination to answer the next three. You are completely on your own for the last two. Be sure to use <u>question</u> marks when you ask the question, <u>exclamation</u> marks when you say something with expression, and <u>quotation</u> marks around exact words said. Question marks and exclamation points will come BEFORE the final quotation marks.

Q: "What did one wall say to the other wall?"
A: "Meet you at the corner!"

Q: "What did the fancy shoe say to the heart?"
A: "You're just a pump!"

Q: "What did the pan say to the egg?"
A: "The yolk's on me!"

Q: "What did the rug say to the floor?"
A: "I've got you covered!"

Q: "What did one banana say to the other banana?"
A: "We've got a peel!"

Q: "What did the curtain rod say to the curtain?"
A: "This is a hold-up!"

Q: "What did the fence say to the fence post?"
A: "You're just a stick-in-the-mud!"

1. **Q:**   "What did one toe say to the other toe?"
   A: _____

2. **Q:**   "What did one candle say to the other candle?"
   A: _____

3. **Q:**   "What did one eye say to the other eye?"
   A: _____

4. **Q:**   _____
   A: _____

5. **Q:**   _____
   A: _____

2-19   **PUNCTUATION RIDDLES**

1. You know there are several thoughts when you see me.
   I have two parts.
   My cousins are periods and commas.
   Who am I?

   _____

2. Time can pass quickly when you see me.
   Although I'm a triplet, something may be missing.
   I always seem to be beside myself.
   Who am I?

   _____

3. You know more information is coming when you see me.
   I am a twin.
   I am under and over myself and can be a body part.
   Who am I?

   _____

4. You'll get the rest of the word after you see me.
   I like to make good connections.
   I am short.
   Who am I?

   _____

5. You expect related information when you see me.
   I am sometimes mistaken for a shorter relative.
   I rhyme with <u>crash</u>.
   Who am I?

   _____

6. You might expect a missing letter when you see me.
   I am sometimes quite possessive.
   I look like my cousin, but I hold a higher position.
   Who am I?

   _____

7. I am straight in writing and slanted in print.
   I need to be emphasized sometimes.
   I might show you a good book title.
   Who am I?

   _____

2-20   UPDATED NURSERY RHYMES

Most of you had fun reading nursery rhymes when you were younger. Now it might be fun to "update" the familiar rhymes with some humorous new twists. Here are a few beginnings. Try your hand at finishing them.

Humpty Dumpty sat on a wall.
It was the coolest place in the mall.

All the _____

_____

_____.

Humpty-Dumpty

Jack Sprat would eat no fat;
His wife was not too lean.

_____

_____.

Mary had a little lamb.
(She really wanted a cat!)

And _____

_____.

Baa, baa, black sheep,
Have you any candy?

_____

_____.

Jack and Jill went up the hill
To look over the other side.

Jack _____

_____

_____.

2-21 COUPLETS: FIND MY BETTER HALF

Two lines that rhyme form couplets. Here are some first halves of couplets; you make up the other (better) half. Words in the RHYME BANK may help you get started, but there are others.

The men who lived up in the tree

_____ .

The ladies in their bright, red sashes

_____ .

The elephants walking one by one

_____ .

The tiger with a great big growl

_____ .

The house that sat upon a hill

_____ .

My bike was just as black as jet

_____ .

RHYME BANK

bee; me; see; tea; be; sea; fee; glee; knee; brie; we; free

ashes; gashes; flashes; trashes; mashes; gnashes; rashes

fun; ton; gun; son; sun; bun; done; nun; pun; run; won

howl; scowl; fowl; foul; jowl; towel; vowel; bowel; dowel

pill; bill; mill; sill; still; fill; will; quill; grill; ill

bet; set; met; let; fret; get; net; pet; vet; regret; wet

2-22   COUPLETS

Between 1927 and 1963 signs advertising Burma-Shave shaving cream amused motorists. The signs displayed humorous couplets divided into five signs spaced at regular distances so each could be seen for about three seconds as motorists passed by.

Below are several examples. Notice the rhythm is fairly consistent (iambic tetrameter). <u>Iambic</u> means the first syllable is <u>un</u>stressed and the second syllable is stressed. <u>Tetrameter</u> means each line has four "feet" or beats. (Some liberties were taken, but this was the general pattern of couplets used.)

After enjoying the signs and analyzing the pattern, write your own couplets on the signs below, using similar rhythm. You don't need to advertise anything, but try to make them as humorous as possible. Don't bother to use punctuation.

WITHIN THIS VALE	**OF** **TOIL**	**AND** **SIN**	**YOUR HEAD GROWS BALD**	**BUT NOT YOUR CHIN**
BEN	**MET ANNA**	**MADE A** **HIT**	**NEGLECTED** **BEARD**	**BEN-ANNA** **SPLIT**
DRIVING **CLOSE**	**TO HIM** **WAS BUNK**	**THEY PULLED HIM**	**OUTTA**	**SOME GUY'S TRUNK**

2-23   LIMERICKS: WHAT'S MY LINE?

Make up a line that fits into the limerick and makes sense. (Okay, the line can make "silly" sense!) In limericks, the last line always rhymes with the first and second lines. The RHYME BANK will help you get started, but should not limit you.

There once was a girl from our school
Who never did follow the rule.
She got in a fix
With all of her tricks

_____.

There once was a boy from Larue
Who had a big hole in his shoe.
He tried as he might
But he never could quite

_____.

There once was a most famous cat
Who always sat on her mat.
She had long grey fur
And a wonderful purr

_____.

There once was a most famous dog
Who always chewed on a log.
He chewed and he chewed
No matter his mood

_____.

© 1996 by The Center for Applied Research in Education

RHYME BANK

fool; fuel; gruel; jewel; mule; cruel; stool; tool; pool

cue; do; goo; hue; voodoo; moo; due; sue; too; new; zoo

at; bat; that; sat; gnat; hat; pat; rat; vat; splat; brat

fog; bog; frog; hog; jog; polliwog; agog; smog; cog; grog

2-24   HANG UP A HAIKU

A haiku is a poem that has three lines. The first and last lines must have 5 syllables; the middle line must have 7. The older haiku poems referred to the seasons of the year, but modern ones have been written about other subjects. Write a haiku about a special holiday. Hang up a haiku by putting one syllable in each piece of clothing on the line.

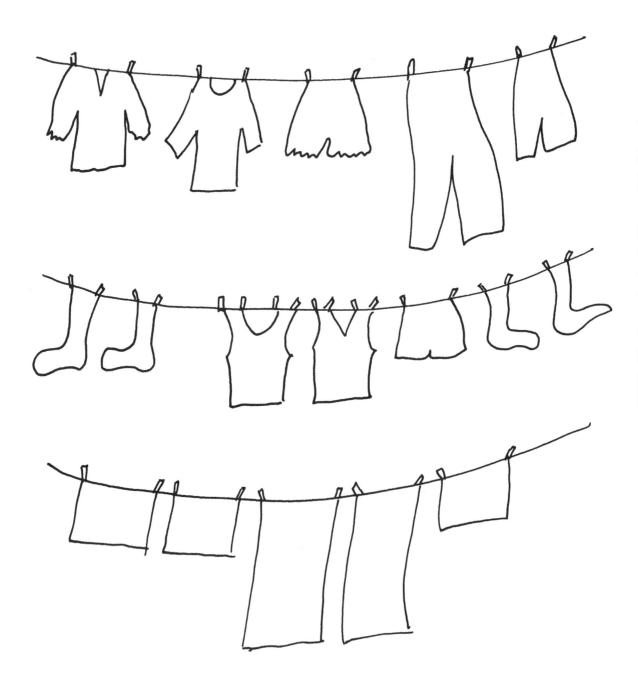

2-25 PARTS OF SPEECH SENTENCE FUN

Divide into rows or teams of eight. Follow the directions by filling in one word as indicated, folding the paper over so the next team member cannot see it, and passing the paper to the next person on your team. At the end, the last person on each team reads the "sentence story" aloud. Students (or teacher) should point out if any word is not used as the correct part of speech. See which team can come up with the most imaginative sentence!

1. adjective   _____

2. adjective   _____

3. noun (person)   _____

4. verb (past tense)   _____

5. preposition   _____

6. adjective   _____

7. noun (place/thing) _____

8. adverb   _____

2-26   RHYME RELAY

Each team uses one sheet of paper like this. Your first team member writes the first line of a poem in this first space provided and passes it on. The second team member writes a RHYMING line in the second space and passes it on. This continues until everyone on your team has participated. You can start again with team member one and go through your team members as long as they can think of new lines, but no member can write out of turn or more than one line at a time. If you cannot think of a line, pass the paper quickly to the next team member. The last one on your team rushes to the front of the room and reads the poem from your team's paper and takes a seat. There is no winner or loser in this game. It is just for fun and to get your creative juices flowing!

1. (new line)

2. (rhyme with line 1)

3. (new line)

4. (rhyme with line 3)

5. (new line)

6. (rhyme with line 5)

7. (new line)

8. (rhyme with line 7)

Start a New Poem Below:

1. (new line)

2. (rhyme with line 1)

3. (new line)

4. (rhyme with line 3)

5. (new line)

6. (rhyme with line 5)

7. (new line)

8. (rhyme with line 7)

2-27   ADD ON

1st Student: When the teacher calls on you, say aloud a simple sentence consisting of

> ONE ARTICLE (a, an, the)
> ONE NOUN (such as man, apple, girl, or other noun)
> ONE ACTION VERB (such as ran, rotted, sat, or other action verb)

Example: *The man ran.*

After you say your sentence to the class, call on a second student.

2nd Student: The second student adds

> ONE ADJECTIVE DESCRIBING THE NOUN (such as tall, old, or other adjective), and says it before the noun.

Example: *The tall man ran.*

After you add your adjective and say your sentence, call on a third student.

3rd Student: The third student adds

> ONE ADVERB DESCRIBING THE VERB (such as quickly, awkwardly, or other adverb) and says it after the verb.

Example: *The tall man ran quickly.*

After you add your adverb and say your sentence, call on a fourth student.

4th Student: The fourth student adds

> ONE PREPOSITIONAL PHRASE DESCRIBING THE VERB (such as down the stairs, up the ladder, or other prepositional phrase) and says it after the adverb.

> **Example:** *The tall man ran quickly down the stairs.*

After you add your prepositional phrase and say your sentence, call on another student who will begin a new simple sentence.

The same procedure continues, with every four students completing a sentence containing an article, a noun, an action verb, an adjective, an adverb, and a prepositional phrase.

2-28   TENSE RELAY

To the Teacher: Pick four teams. The goal of the relay is to introduce, practice, or review verb tenses. You put the following on the chalkboard, using four distinct columns:

PRESENT TENSE	PAST TENSE	FUTURE TENSE	PERFECT TENSES
Today I	Yesterday I	Tomorrow I will or shall	I have, had, will have, or shall have
SEE	SAW	SEE	SEEN

Number of Players: Entire class

Materials Needed: Both regular and irregular verbs can be used for the relay. The next page shows COMMON IRREGULAR VERBS LIST with four tenses. You can reproduce it as a study list for students or use it as a quick check sheet for yourself as the game progresses.

How to Play: The first student on the first team rushes to the chalkboard, puts any present tense verb under column 1, and returns to seat. The first student on the next team hurries to chalkboard, puts correct *past* tense of that same verb under column 2, and is seated. The first person on the third team does the same for the *future tense;* the first person on the fourth team puts up the *perfect tense.* Then the second person on the first team has a turn, and so on with each team sending up its next member.

No player can stand up or head for the board until the previous player is seated. (This avoids confusion and gives everyone a fair chance.) When errors are made, the student (or students if several miss sequentially) stand up for a moment. As soon as a child gets the correct answer, the player "captures" the standing student or students for his or her team. Thus, the less able pupils still have value to the team, because the relay team with the most players at the end of the time period is the winner.

Rationale: Instead of being "out," less able players continue to get practice and be actively engaged. In fact, errors make the relay more interesting because different teams end up doing various tenses, instead of the first team always introducing new words, the second team doing the past tense, and so forth.

Modifications: Fourth or fifth graders may want to do just present, past, and future tenses. Sixth graders should be able to include the perfect tenses. If you use three tenses, of course you will use three teams instead of four. With less able children, you might use just present and past tenses. Two tenses can be played with four teams, with the remaining procedures staying the same. Another modification would be to use *Present Participle* and *Past Participle* as categories. The game can be adapted to whatever you are teaching about tenses.

© 1996 by The Center for Applied Research in Education

COMMON IRREGULAR VERBS LIST

(for use with TENSE RELAY)

PRESENT	PAST	FUTURE (will or shall)	PERFECT (have, has, had, will have, or shall have)
am	was	be	been
begin	began	begin	begun
blow	blew	blow	blown
bring	brought	bring	brought
build	built	build	built
burst	burst	burst	burst
buy	bought	buy	bought
catch	caught	catch	caught
choose	chose	choose	chosen
come	came	come	come
do	did	do	done
drink	drank	drink	drunk
drive	drove	drive	driven
eat	ate	eat	eaten
fall	fell	fall	fallen
feel	felt	feel	felt
fight	fought	fight	fought
fly	flew	fly	flown
forget	forgot	forget	forgotten
freeze	froze	freeze	frozen
give	gave	give	given
go	went	go	gone
grow	grew	grow	grown
hang	hung	hang	hanged
have	had	have	had
hear	heard	hear	heard
hit	hit	hit	hit
hold	held	hold	held
keep	kept	keep	kept
know	knew	know	known
lose	lost	lose	lost
ring	rang	ring	rung
rise	rose	rise	risen
say	said	say	said
see	saw	see	seen
sell	sold	sell	sold
shake	shook	shake	shaken
sing	sang	sing	sung
sit	sat	sit	sat
steal	stole	steal	stolen
stink	stank	stink	stunk
take	took	take	taken
teach	taught	teach	taught
tear	tore	tear	torn
tell	told	tell	told
think	thought	think	thought

SIMPLIFIED GRAMMAR GAME

To the Teacher: Copy one sheet of four cards for each player. Cut sheets apart or have students cut them apart. (An alternative is to use a felt pen to mark the words on 3″ × 5″ index cards. One pack of 100 index cards services 25 students.) Only *you* will need the list of words.

Distribute one set of four SIMPLIFIED GRAMMAR (CARDS) to each student. Read the SIMPLIFIED GRAMMAR (WORDS) in order, allowing time for students to raise their cards identifying what kind of word each is before going on to the next word. Glance around the class to see how they are doing, and give a brief explanation of the correct answer, if needed.

Number of Players: Entire class

Materials Needed: • SIMPLIFIED GRAMMAR (CARDS)—1 set of 4 for each student

                • SIMPLIFIED GRAMMAR (WORDS)—1 copy

How to Play: Read words. Students raise correct flash card, giving themselves one point for each correct answer. Once a student raises a card, he or she cannot change his or her answer.

Rationale: This is basically for practice. It encourages fast thinking, focus on attention, and a small amount of competition, though since they keep their own scores, students are really playing against themselves, rather than their classmates. They do not need to reveal their scores to anyone if they don't want to, so those who do well can gain esteem, but those who don't do so well can keep practicing until they get better at it. There is immediate reinforcement of correct answers, so even if a student "misses," he or she continues to learn.

Modifications: Students can be given the list of words and asked to put 1 (for Who or What); 2 (for Action Verb); 3 (for Prepositional Phrase); or 4 (for Adverb) before each word on the list. Most students prefer the game version, however.

SIMPLIFIED GRAMMAR (WORDS)

1. brother
2. carefully
3. at school
4. slowly
5. Chris
6. in the park
7. stuffed
8. skillfully
9. dented
10. below the dashboard
11. crowd
12. crazily
13. voted
14. elephant
15. stubbornly
16. committee
17. hogs
18. hopped
19. raced
20. down the road
21. swallowed
22. sister
23. sweater
24. counted
25. over the car

26. parents
27. jumped
28. on the bench
29. honesty
30. garbled
31. friends
32. wobbled
33. around the bend
34. under the huge tent
35. noisily
36. apples
37. sheepishly
38. gracefully
39. underneath the tree
40. New York City
41. Empire State Building
42. bit
43. into the river
44. stood
45. group
46. quickly
47. in my room
48. up his nose
49. quietly
50. into the garbage

WHO/WHAT
(noun)

HOW
(adverb)

ACTION
(verb)

WHERE
(prepositional phrase)

CANNED SENTENCES GAME

To the Teacher: Run off one copy of CANNED SENTENCES GAME (WORDS). Cut each word or phrase into a separate strip of paper. Put all the subject strips (column 1 words) into Can 1; all the verb strips (column 2 words) into Can 2; all adverb strips (column 3 words) into Can 3.

Number of Players: Entire class

Materials Needed: • Three cans or containers

• CANNED SENTENCES GAME (WORDS)—1 copy

How to Play: Students draw a word or phrase from each can and read their sentences to the class. They will all be complete sentences. Be sure students read them in order (Can 1, Can 2, Can 3).

Rationale: Some sentences will be silly, and that's why students enjoy the fun of the CANNED SENTENCES GAME while they familiarize themselves with basic sentence structure. They especially like it when an unlikely verb or adverb comes up with "best friend," "our teacher," or "the principal" as the subject!

Modifications: If cans are not available, any container can be used. Additionally, students often like to contribute their own words to the cans. This can *really* get interesting!

Canned Sentences Game (Words)

CAN 1 (SUBJECTS)	CAN 2 (VERBS)	CAN 3 (ADVERBS)
my best friend	gargled	carelessly
the elephant	wobbled	crazily
the old man	laughed	loudly
the young lady	hiccupped	boldly
the squirrel	staggered	dizzily
my pet raccoon	gobbled	dangerously
my father	ran	carefully
my mother	skipped	brazenly
my new car	hopped	shyly
our green tree	jumped	lovingly
the neighbor	swayed	well
our teacher	acted	tearfully
the principal	scratched	cheerfully
our cook	played	sadly
my baby sister	worked	happily
my baby brother	sped	strangely
my heart	skied	oddly
my leg	skated	superhumanly
my grandfather	rollerbladed	stubbornly
my grandmother	drove	quietly
my bicycle	pounded	skillfully
my doll	cried	stupidly
the train	wept	rapidly
the airline	crashed	awkwardly
the turkey	chugged	repeatedly

2-31 GOOFBALLS GAME

To the Teacher: Make one copy of GOOFBALLS (PHRASES), cutting each beginning and ending into separate slips of paper. (The first page will accommodate 28 students; the next page will handle 26 students.) Be sure each student has a slip of paper and therefore a partner. All goofballs should be read aloud at some point. When partners are ascertained. have the partnership write its own goofballs and read them to the class.

If *you* want to choose partners, pass out slips with one half of each goofball to the individuals you want to pair; if you want to do it randomly, pass the halves out at random. If students need an active, noisy activity, let them wander around and find their matching half; if you want a more orderly activity, let students take turns reading their half and the corresponding "other half" can raise their hand to read the last part. In any case, make sure everyone hears each goofball before they try to create their own.

Some pairs will not be able to think up any original goofballs; usually other pairs get "on a roll" and make up several. There should be no penalty for not coming up with a goofball, but do not tell students that ahead of time or they may just "talk" instead of wracking their brains and making a decent effort. When finished, have students read their own goofballs.

Number of Players: Entire class

Materials Needed: • GOOFBALLS (PHRASES)—1 copy

How to Play:
1. Find the person with the other half of the goofball.
2. Prepare to read it to the class.
3. Write your own goofballs in partnership or alone.
4. Prepare to share them with the class.

Rationale: GOOFBALLS are based on the old "moron jokes," but changed to make them genderless and not offensive to slower students. Kids seem to love these, so expect laughter or groans, depending on the particular class makeup. Making up their own goofballs helps them develop imagination and can be a good introduction to the concept of puns. Creativity and a sense of humor often do not come automatically; this activity can provide stimuli to help students develop these abilities.

GOOFBALLS (PHRASES)

Did You Hear About the Goofball Who:

Drank iodine	so it'd dream in technicolor
Ran around the bed	so it could catch some sleep
Went to a football game	so it could get a quarterback
Stayed up all night	to study for a blood test
Wouldn't pay bus fare	because its name was Crime and crime never pays
Disobeyed "halt" orders	because its name was Time and time marches on
Filled the gym with water	because the coach told it that it was going to be a sub
Put its nose out the window	so the wind would blow it
Thought the bed was too narrow	so it put on a bed spread
Pulled its teeth out	so it could have gum to chew
Jumped through a screen	and strained itself
Drank eight colas	and burped 7-Up®
Saluted the refrigerator	because it was General Electric
Thought it was built upside down	because its nose ran and its feet smelled

GOOFBALLS (PHRASES)
(cont'd)

Did You Hear About the Goofball Who:

Didn't want to die	so it stayed in the living room
Invented spaghetti	by getting it out of its noodle
Wanted to be a vitamin	because it heard someone say, "Vitamin B-1"
Ran around a box top	because it said, "Tear around here"
Was very shy	so it went into the bedroom to change its mind
Was locked out of its house	so it ran around until it was all in
Backed off the bus	so nobody would grab its seat
Cut off its fingers	because it played piano by ear
Ate bullets	so it could have bangs
Put crackers in its shoes	to feed its pigeon toes
Put iodine on its paycheck	because it got a salary cut
Golfed with two pairs of socks	in case it got a hole in one
Died with its boots on	so it wouldn't hurt its toes when it kicked the bucket

Section Three

READING AND
LITERATURE

3-1 SCATTERGORIZE

A category is a group of items that have something in common. The items below are in alphabetical order instead of by category. Unscatter the words and write them on the blanks under the proper categories.

Hint: You will not use all the blanks in some categories.

alligator	January	pigeon
April	July	pony
August	June	Saturday
burro	lamb	September
calf	March	squirrel
cattle	May	Sunday
chipmunk	Monday	Thursday
December	monkey	Tuesday
February	November	turkey
Friday	October	Wednesday

MONTHS   **DAYS OF WEEK**   **ANIMALS**

_____   _____   _____

_____   _____   _____

_____   _____   _____

_____   _____   _____

_____   _____   _____

_____   _____   _____

_____   _____   _____

_____   _____   _____

_____   _____   _____

_____   _____   _____

_____   _____   _____

3-2   SAFETY FIRST

The numbered words and phrases are necessary to recognize either for your safety or to avoid embarrassment. Put the NUMBER of each item on the lines under the proper categories. If you get them all correct, the total of each column will be equal.

PHYSICAL SAFETY

_____
_____
_____
_____
_____
_____
_____
_____
_____
_____

TOTAL _____

AVOIDANCE OF EMBARRASSMENT

_____
_____
_____
_____
_____
_____
_____
_____
_____
_____

TOTAL _____

1. Employees only
2. Antidote
3. Caution
4. Combustible
5. Dynamite
6. This end up
7. Private property
8. Poison
9. Explosives
10. External use only

11. Out of order
12. Contaminated
13. Ladies
14. Use other door
15. High voltage
16. Gentlemen
17. Flammable
18. Private entrance
19. No admittance
20. Do not inhale fumes

3-3   IT'S ABOUT TIME

Four common time zones are shown below. When it is a certain hour in New York, it is one hour earlier in Houston, two hours earlier in Denver, and three hours earlier in Los Angeles. Fill in the rest of the first grid using that information as your guide.

Then, in the second grid, take time out for spelling the numbers you used. The asterisks show no letters are needed there.

Eastern	Central	Mountain	Pacific
NEW YORK	HOUSTON	DENVER	LOS ANGELES
1			
	11		
		9	
			7

Time Out for Spelling:

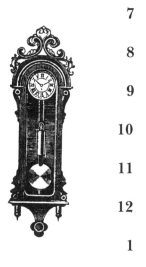

7	*	*		e				*
8	*	*	*	e				
9				e	*	*	*	*
10	*	*		e		*	*	*
11	*			e				*
12	*			e				*
1	*			e	*	*	*	*

3-4 AUTHOR! AUTHOR!

1. Arrange these blocks in the diagram below to form a famous older author.

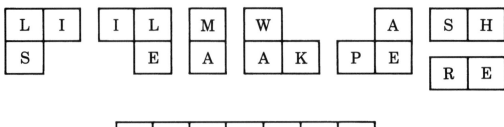

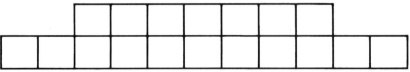

2. Can you name any works by this author?

_____

_____

3. Arrange these blocks in the diagram below to form a famous modern author.

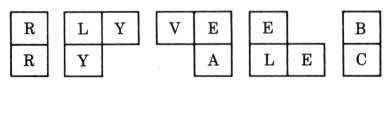

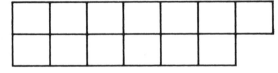

4. Can you name any works by this author?

_____

_____

Name _____

3-5   PSEUDONYMS

A pseudonym is a name someone uses instead of the actual birth name. Writers often use pseudonyms to disguise themselves or because their own name is hard to remember. Match these rhyming clues to the names of the real authors.

PEN NAMES	REAL NAMES	RHYME CLUE TO NAME
1. Poor Richard	_____	Hen Pranklin
2. Boz	_____	Carls Pickens
3. Ellis Bell	_____	Jemily Fontee
4. Lewis Carroll	_____	Carls Podgson
5. Mark Twain	_____	Pamyule Lemons
6. Mary Westmacott	_____	Sagatha Misty
7. Nicholas Blake	_____	Heesul Pay-Dewus
8. Elia	_____	Carls Ham
9. George Eliot	_____	Kerry Pan Heavens
10. George Orwell	_____	Hairic Stare

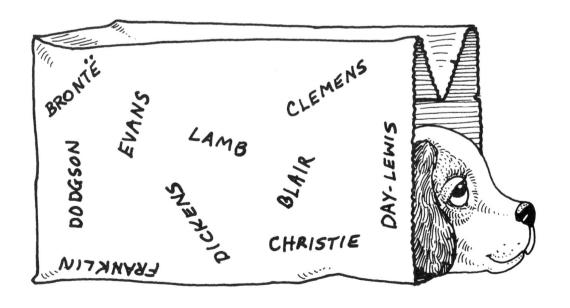

107

3-6   GO FOR THE GOLD

Some books or characters sparkle with gold, silver, or bronze. Fill in the right colors in these major book titles or characters. Be sure to use a capital letter at the beginning of each word.

1. _____ on the Tree

2. Samurai of _____ Hill

3. The _____ Sword

4. Long John _____

5. _____ ilocks

6. The Goose that Laid the _____ en Eggs

7. The _____ Skates

8. _____ Days

9. Otto of the _____ Hand

10. The _____ Bow

11. The _____ en Bird

12. The _____ Bug

13. Good as _____

14. The _____ en Bowl

Hint: There are 7 GOLD, 6 SILVER, and 1 BRONZE.

108

© 1996 by The Center for Applied Research in Education

3-7   IN BLACK AND WHITE

What is black and white and "red" all over? Why, <u>books,</u> of course! See how many book titles or characters you can fill in with the color of black or white in their titles. Be sure to use a capital letter at the beginning of each word. **Hint:** 13 B; 10 W.

1. _____ <u>Hearts in Battersea</u> (Joan Aiken)

2. _____ <u>Beauty</u> (Anna Sewell)

3. _____ Knight (from <u>Through the Looking Glass</u>)

4. _____ Rabbit (from Alice's adventures)

5. _____ <u>Jack</u> (Leon Garfield)

6. _____ <u>Pearl</u> (Scott O'Dell)

7. _____ <u>Like Me</u> (John H. Griffin)

8. _____ <u>Boy</u> (Richard Wright)

9. _____ <u>Fang</u> (Jack London)

10. _____ <u>Star, Bright Dawn</u> (Scott O'Dell)

11. _____ <u>Sheep</u> (from nursery rhyme)

12. _____-<u>Jacket</u> (Herman Melville)

13. _____ <u>Gold</u> (Marguerite Henry)

14. _____ <u>Horses</u> (Luigi Pirandello)

15. _____ <u>Stallion of Lipizza</u> (Marguerite Henry)

16. <u>The</u> _____ <u>Snake</u> (fairy tale)

17. <u>The</u> _____ <u>Cat</u> (Edgar Allan Poe)

18. <u>The</u> _____ <u>Seal</u> (Rudyard Kipling)

19. <u>The</u> _____ <u>Cat</u> (W. W. Jacobs)

20. <u>The</u> _____ <u>Stallion</u> (Walter Farley)

21. <u>The</u> _____ <u>Arrow</u> (Robert Louis Stevenson)

22. <u>Snow</u> _____ (fairy tale)

23. <u>Pangur Ban, the</u> _____ <u>Cat</u> (Fay Sampson)

3-8   READING COUNTS

These titles contain numbers or words relating to numbers. See if you can make your reading count. Authors are in parentheses.

1. _____ Fat Summer (Robert Litsyte)

2. The House of _____ Fathers (Meindert DeJong)

3. Journey to an _____ Number (E. L. Konigsburg)

4. The _____ Hats of Bartholomew Cubbins (Theodore Geisel)

5. _____ of Cats (Wanda Gag)

6. Hitty: Her First _____ Years (Rachel Field)

7. Just _____ Friend (Lynn Hall)

8. A Tale of _____ Cities (Charles Dickens)

9. The _____ Musketeers (Alexandre Dumas)

10. Cheaper by the _____ (F. Gilbreth and E. Carey)

11. _____ Years Before the Mast (Richard Dana)

12. Catch-_____ (Joseph Heller)

13. The _____ Steps (John Buchan)

14. Around the World in _____ Days (Jules Verne)

15. _____ Leagues Under the Sea (Jules Verne)

16. _____ (George Orwell)

17. Fahrenheit _____ (Ray Bradbury)

18. The House of _____ Gables (Nathaniel Hawthorne)

19. _____ Cousins (Louisa May Alcott)

20. Ivanov _____ (Elizabeth Janeway)

21. _____ Against the Dealer (Cynthia Voigt)

Hints: #2 + #13 + #7 = #6
#21 − #19 = #18 + #8
#1 + #9 = #10 − #19

3-9   BOOK OR STORY CHARACTERS

Can you identify these book or story characters from the clues?

1. HOrobOD

1. _____

2.  SIL VER

2. _____

3.

3. _____

4.

4. _____

5.

5. _____

6.  c

6. _____

7. MY

7. _____

8. mos

8. _____

3-10   ALL ABOUT BOOKS

The following rhymes give you clues to the parts of a book and other words you need to know about books. Use the BOOK WORDS to help you figure them out, and write the answers on the lines.

1. I pen the words
   to make life brighter.
   I am the author;

   I am the _____.

2. If I am talented,
   the book is greater.
   I draw the pictures;

   I'm the _____.

3. I'm like a dictionary
   of words. Yes, siree!
   I'm in the back;

   I'm the _____.

4. When a book comes out,
   it's a special occasion.
   This number shows

   Date of _____.

5. Near the beginning,
   a special stage
   for the name of the book,

   I'm the _____ page.

BOOK WORDS

publication   writer   title   glossary   illustrator

3-11   PARTS OF A BOOK

The following rhymes give you clues to the parts of a book and other words you need to know about books. Use the PARTS STORE to help you figure them out, and write the answers on the lines.

1. The words you see
   are very vital.
   They say my name.

   I am the ___ ___ ___ ___ ___ .

2. You see me on the shelf,
   looking tall and fine,
   with call numbers on me.

   I am the ___ ___ ___ ___ ___ .

3. I am a pair,
   one side, another;
   Filled with pages,

   I am the ___ ___ ___ ___ ___ .

4. I put things in order,
   and make common sense
   out of what is inside.

   I'm the Table of ___ ___ ___ ___ ___ ___ ___ ___ .

5. If I were absent,
   you'd all be wrecks—
   I show the subjects;

   I am the ___ ___ ___ ___ ___ .

PARTS STORE

index	spine	contents	title	cover

3-12   STORY PUZZLE

Answer the questions. Cross out the letters in your answer that correspond to each row. Put the remaining letters below.

Row 1	S	R	T	H	H	E	O	E
Row 2	C	S	T	T	E	L	O	A
Row 3	A	N	S	M	A	R	O	T
Row 4	O	R	P	I	I	E	G	S
Row 5	A	K	G	N	I	P	L	I
Row 6	R	H	R	R	A	T	E	I
Row 7	Y	L	E	L	B	F	I	A
Row 8	T	B	A	I	U	L	W	N
Row 9	O	N	H	U	C	R	G	I
Row 10	T	I	C	S	K	R	E	C

Books make the best furniture.

1. Who was <u>Misty of Chincoteague?</u> _____

2. Who wrote <u>Little Women?</u> _____

3. Who was "the pest"? _____

4. What was Wilbur of <u>Charlotte's Web?</u> _____

5. Who wrote <u>The Jungle Book?</u> _____

6. Who was "the spy"? _____

7. What boy "ate fried worms"? _____

8. Who wrote <u>Huckleberry Finn?</u> _____

9. Who stole Christmas? _____

10. What was in "Times Square"? _____

— — — —   — — — — — — — —

— — — —   — — — — — — — — — —!

Name _____

3-13   NEWBERY AWARD BOOKS

The Newbery Award is given each year to an author of a distinguished piece of literature for children. Use the clues to identify these outstanding Newbery Award books. How many of them have you read? If not all, better get going!

1. S
    A
    R
    A
    H

2. Hero +

3. Days Days Days
        Days   Days
    Days Days Days

4. 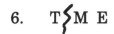 → Terabithia

5. ┌─────────┐
    │   │
    │ King   │
    │   │
    │   │
    │   │
    └─────────┘

6. T ⌇ M E

7.  J
                       o
                       h
                       n

8.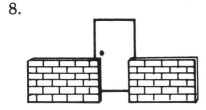

1. _____

   _____

2. _____

   _____

3. _____

   _____

4. _____

5. _____

   _____

6. _____

7. _____

   _____

8. _____

   _____

115

3-14   IDIOMS

An idiom is a group of words with a meaning different than the literal meaning of the words. In this story the literal meanings are underlined. Substitute the correct idioms on the lines with the corresponding numbers below. Use the IDIOM BANK to help you.

IDIOM BANK

all thumbs	trick up his sleeve	drives me crazy
cracks me up	nose buried in a book	end of my rope
cut corners	jumped out of his skin	in the doghouse
tickled pink	opened a can of worms	lend me a hand
blew his stack	on pins and needles	splitting headache

I asked my friend to (1) <u>temporarily give me an extremity</u> because it (2) <u>propels me forward to insanity</u> to be (3) <u>entirely the smallest digit</u> when doing a project. I was at the (4) <u>finish of my entwined sisal.</u> I like to do things right and not (5) <u>slice where the edges meet.</u>

My friend had his (6) <u>proboscis entombed in a printed volume</u> and nearly (7) <u>leaped on one foot out of his epidermis</u> when I startled him! (8) He <u>moved the air in his chimney</u> and I thought I was really (9) <u>in the canine dwelling.</u> I waited (10) <u>on sewing paraphernalia</u> until he said he'd help me.

I thought I had (11) <u>uncovered a container of segmented crawlers,</u> but he had a (12) <u>stunt up the clothing that covered his arm.</u> Instead of ending up with a (13) <u>separating pain in the cranium,</u> I was (14) <u>pleased a pale red</u> when we finished. It still (15) <u>severs me to a higher position</u> when I think about that day!

1. _____
2. _____
3. _____
4. _____
5. _____
6. _____
7. _____
8. _____

9. _____
10. _____
11. _____
12. _____
13. _____
14. _____
15. _____

3-15   KNOW YOUR BODY LANGUAGE

Sometimes we communicate with our body instead of words. Other times, we use words taken from parts of the body to express ourselves in metaphor. The definitions below describe words that contain one or more body parts used figuratively. Use the BODY PARTS MORGUE to see how many you can write in the proper blanks.

1. You are _____ and _____ above the rest (*way above*).

2. You are going to have to _____ the bill (*pay for*).

3. You haven't got a _____ to stand on (*any excuse*).

4. The answer is on the tip of my _____ (*almost coming out*).

5. I have a green _____ (*good gardener*).

6. This is a meal to sink my _____ into (*really enjoy*).

7. I had butterflies in my _____ (*was really nervous*).

8. We rubbed _____ with the top guests (*socialized with*).

9. We see _____ to _____ (*agree*).

10. He had to _____ the music (*take the consequences*).

11. She worked her _____ to the bone (*worked hard*).

12. The manager jumped down her _____ (*yelled at her*).

13. The coach told us to keep on our _____ (*stay alert*).

14. Jane won the race by a _____ (*very small margin*).

15. Our team brought our opponents to their _____ (*won big*).

BODY PARTS MORGUE

face	thumb	stomach	foot	toes	eye	eye
head	shoulders	teeth	tongue	elbows	knees
	leg	nose	fingers	throat	

Name _____

3-16   TEST YOUR LOGIC

Four athletic girls met at a basketball game. They were from different cities, each played a different sport, and no two wore the same color uniform. Given the clues below, fill in the chart so each girl is matched with her city, sport, and uniform color.

	CHRIS	MARIA	BABETTE	KENDALEE
CITY				
SPORT				
COLOR				

1. Kendalee wears a red uniform.

2. The girl with the blue uniform likes to play golf.

3. Babette likes to play baseball.

4. Maria is from New York.

5. The girl who wears the blue uniform is not from New York.

6. Someone plays basketball, but she doesn't wear yellow.

7. Babette is not from Detroit.

8. The girl in green does not run track, but another girl does.

9. Chris is from Pittsburgh.

10. The girl with the yellow uniform is from San Francisco.

3-17   COMMON PROVERBS LIST

A bird in the hand is worth two in the bush.
A good book is the best companion.
A man is known by the company he keeps.
A penny saved is a penny earned.
A place for everything and everything in its place.
A rotten apple spoils the barrel.
A stitch in time saves nine.
A watched pot never boils.
Absence makes the heart grow fonder.
Actions speak louder than words.
After the storm comes the calm.
All that glitters is not gold.
All good things come in small packages.
All good things must come to an end.
All's well that ends well.
An apple a day keeps the doctor away.
An ounce of prevention is worth a pound of cure.
April showers bring May flowers.
As the twig is bent, so the tree will grow.
Beauty is only skin deep.
Better late than never.
Better to be safe than sorry.
Birds of a feather flock together.
Blood is thicker than water.
Clothes don't make the man.
Do unto others as you would have them do unto you.
Don't buy a pig in a poke.
Don't count your chickens before they're hatched.
Don't cross a bridge until you come to it.
Don't cry over spilt milk.
Don't cut off your nose to spite your face.
Don't give up the ship.
Don't judge a book by its cover.
Don't put all your eggs in one basket.
Don't put the cart before the horse.
Don't put off until tomorrow what you can do today.
Don't rob Peter to pay Paul.
Don't try to lock the barn after the horses are stolen.
Easy come, easy go.
Every cloud has a silver lining.
Every rose has its thorn.
Experience is the best teacher.
Forewarned is forearmed.
God helps those who help themselves.
Great oaks from little acorns grow.
Half a loaf is better than none.
Handsome is as handsome does.
He who hesitates is lost.
Health is better than wealth.
Honesty is the best policy.
Idle hands are the devil's workshop.
If wishes were horses, beggars would ride.

3-17   Common Proverbs List
(cont'd)

If at first you don't succeed, try, try again.
If the shoe fits, put it on.
It never rains but what it pours.
It takes two to make a quarrel.
It's an ill wind that blows nobody good.
It's easier said than done.
It's never too late to learn.
Jack of all trades, master of none.
Let sleeping dogs lie.
Lie down with dogs; get up with fleas.
Like father, like son.
Look before you leap.
Many a true word is spoken in jest.
Marry in haste and repent at leisure.
Misery loves company.
Money is the root of all evil.
Never bite off more than you can chew.
Never make a mountain out of a molehill.
Nothing ventured, nothing gained.
One good turn deserves another.
One man's meat is another man's poison.
Opposites attract.
Out of the frying pan, into the fire.
Overcome evil with good.
Paddle your own canoe.
People who live in glass houses shouldn't throw stones.
Practice makes perfect.
Practice what you preach.
Silence is golden.
Strike while the iron is hot.
Talk is cheap.
The darkest hour comes before the dawn.
The early bird catches the worm.
The pen is mightier than the sword.
The proof of the pudding is in the eating.
They can because they think they can.
Too many cooks spoil the broth.
Truth is stranger than fiction.
Turn about is fair play.
Two heads are better than one.
Two wrongs don't make a right.
United we stand, divided we fall.
Waste not, want not.
Whatever is worth doing at all is worth doing well.
When one door shuts, another opens.
When the cat's away, the mice will play.
Where there's a will, there's a way.
Where there's smoke, there's fire.
You can lead a horse to water, but you can't make him drink.
You can't have your cake and eat it, too.
You catch more flies with honey than with vinegar.
You make your bed; you must lie on it.

3-18   PROVERBS FUN

Fill in the missing letters to form common proverbs.

____ ____   1. A bid in the hand is worth two in the bus.

____ ____   2. You catch more lies with hone than vinegar.

____ ____   3. Practice hat you reach.

____ ____   4. All that litters is not old.

____ ____   5. Half a oaf is better than one.

____   6. April showers ring May flowers.

____ ____   7. It's ever too late to earn.

____   8. Beauty is only kin deep.

____ ____   9. Better ate than ever.

____ ____   10. Bids of a feather lock together.

____ ____   11. Don't cut off your nose to spit your ace.

____   12. If the hoe fits, put it on.

____   13. Don't give up the hip.

____ ____   14. Great oaks from little corns row.

____ ____   15. All god things come in mall packages.

____ ____   16. Don't put the art before the hose.

____ ____   17. As the wig is bent, so the tree will row.

____ ____   18. Never bit off more than you can hew.

____ ____   19. Out of the frying pa, into the ire.

____   20. The pen is mightier than the word.

____ ____   21. Turn about is air lay.

____ ____   22. A watched pot ever oils.

____ ____   23. When one door huts, another pens.

____ ____   24. A lace for everything and everything in its lace.

____   25. Actions peak louder than words.

3-19   PROVERBS BY FIRST LETTERS

Try to figure out the proverbs with the clues below. The first letter of each word in the proverb is given. Your teacher <u>may</u> let you use the COMMON PROVERBS LIST to help you. Write the proverbs on the lines.

1. A   p   s   i   a   p   e.

   _____

   _____

2. I   a   f   y   d   s,   t,   t   a.

   _____

   _____

3. O   o   t   f   p,   i   t   f.

   _____

   _____

4. T   i   c.

   _____

   _____

5. D   c   o   s   m.

   _____

   _____

6. D   t   t   l   t   b   a   t   h   a   s.

   _____

   _____

7. H   i   a   h   d.

   _____

   _____

3-20   CODED PROVERBS

Use clues and codes to find proverbs that fit. Write the correct proverb on the line below each code.

To the Teacher: Hand out COMMON PROVERBS LIST, if desired.

1. /   / / / /   / / / /   / / / / / / / / /   / / / / / / / /.

_____

2. VCCVCCV   CVCVC   CCV CVVCC   CCVC CVCCVC.

_____

3. Bmm't xfmm uibu foet xfmm.

_____

4. W _ _ _ e t _ _ _ _ ' _ _ _ _ _ _,   t _ _ _ _ ' _ _ _ _ _ _.

_____

5.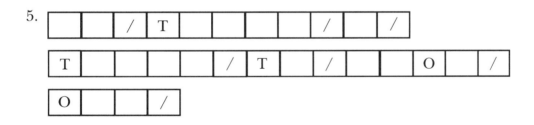

6. ASTITCHINTIMESAVESNINE.

_____

7. Dadpel oury now ceona.

_____

3-21 PROVERB OPPOSITES

Most proverbs are meaningful comments on life, but sometimes well-known proverbs contradict each other. Then what's a person to do? Look at the COMMON PROVERBS LIST and find at least five pairs that give us opposite views.

Example: You're never too old to learn.
                 You can't teach an old dog new tricks.

1. _____

_____

2. _____

_____

3. _____

_____

4. _____

_____

5. _____

_____

BONUS: Can you find others on the list or think of proverbs you are familiar with that contradict each other?

_____

_____

_____

_____

3-22   MIXED-UP PROVERBS

The following statements are made up of parts of proverbs. See if you can sort the mixed-up proverbs by adding the correct beginnings and endings. You should have fourteen common proverbs when you finish.

1. One man's meat / is worth a pound of cure.

_____

_____

2. Lie down with dogs / when the cat's away.

_____

_____

3. A rotten apple / catches the worm.

_____

_____

4. Fools rush in / before they are hatched.

_____

_____

5. Misery loves / a fool and his money.

_____

_____

6. Every rose / has a silver lining.

_____

_____

7. You can't have your cake and / lie on it.

_____

_____

3-23   PROVERB SQUARES

Put the letters from balloon #1 into the squares under #1. Continue with balloon #2 and so on until all squares are filled.

The challenge is to put the letters in the correct <u>order</u> so that they will spell out a famous proverb when read from left to right. Your teacher <u>may</u> offer a list of proverbs to help you.

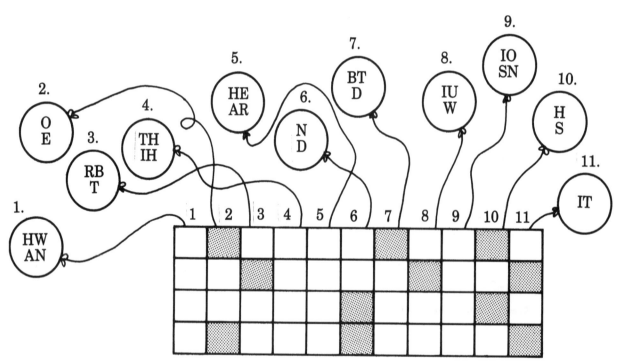

Proverb: _____

_____

3-24   PROVERB PATHS

Each large rectangle contains a common proverb. To find it you must start at the beginning and go to the end in a winding path. The beginning letter of each new word is circled. Every letter will be next to the next letter (either up, down, or diagonally) and you will never cross your path. There will be extra letters. The number of letters in each word is shown to help you as you fill in the proverb in the blanks provided.

1.

O	A	C	N	A
R	(B)	K	F	(L)
E	D	O	O	H
T	F	O	O	I
O	R	(Y)	U	K
S	E	E	(L)	N
Y	A	G	P	U
A	P	J	R	Q

← **Begin**

End (↑ below A in first column area)

L

__ __ __ __

__ __ __ __ __ __

__ __ __

__ __ __ __ .

2.   **Begin** →

(O)	F	F	R	T
B	V	E	C	R
A	D	O	N	A
I	V	T	M	Y
L	O	(E)	E	X
I	(W)	(G)	O	H
T	H	K	O	S
J	P	D	R	U

↑ (End)

O

__ __ __ __ __ __ __ __

__ __ __ __

__ __ __ __

__ __ __ __ .

3-25   PROVERBS BY KEY WORDS

Can you identify famous proverbs by a key word? Write the proverbs on the lines provided. Your teacher <u>may</u> allow you to use the COMMON PROVERBS LIST to help you.

1. | P | E | T | E | R |

_____

_____

2. | E | A | S | Y |

_____

_____

3. | H | E | S | I | T | A | T | E | S |

_____

_____

4. | J | A | C | K |

_____

_____

5. | N | O | T | H | I | N | G |

_____

_____

6. | M | O | L | E | H | I | L | L |

_____

_____

7. | C | O | O | K | S |

_____

_____

3-26   CAN YOU IDENTIFY THESE PROVERBS?

See if you can add up the clues to find famous proverbs. Your teacher <u>may</u> let you use a list of proverbs to help you.

1.

1. _____
_____

2. cleanlinessgodliness

2. _____
_____

3. TIstichME saves 9

3. _____
_____

4. **BLOOD** WATER

4. _____

5. Rbetterthan

5. _____
_____

6.

6. _____
_____

7.

7. _____
_____

3-27 COUPLETS GAME

Number of Players: 2

Materials Needed:
- Spinner
- Game board (below)
- Markers

How to Play: Spin spinner. Go forward the number of spaces indicated. Write a couplet that ends with the rhyming words you land on. Take turns until a winner arrives at the END. More than one player can occupy the same space.

If a player cannot come up with a couplet quickly, the turn is lost, and the player must go back to the previous position. The other player then takes a turn. At the end of the game, read your couplets to the class.

fog frog		moan stone	three knee	tale sale	run fun
caught fought		snow blow			room broom
car mar		ring king		THE END	side wide
pin win		nine fine			
hole mole		night light	trap clap	green queen	grade made
book crook					man van
burn learn	time crime	list hissed	five dive	six kicks	ten pen

Variation: Ask your teacher if you can rhyme the couplets orally. In some cases, the teacher may allow it, depending on the classroom situation.

3-28 TRITE SIMILES INSTRUCTIONS

To the Teacher: The next three pages contain trite similes, two pages including the word <u>as</u> and one page including the word <u>like</u> to be used with SIMILES PARTNERSHIP and SIMILES GAME.

1. Copy the pages on tagboard and laminate, if feasible, or make the pages into plastic transparencies.

2. Cut cards apart with paper cutter, being sure all cards are of uniform size.

3. After similes are separated from each other, cut each individual simile into two parts, with the beginning on one part and the ending on the other. MAKE SURE TO KEEP ALL THE BEGINNINGS TOGETHER IN ONE PILE. MAKE SURE TO KEEP ALL THE ENDINGS TOGETHER IN ANOTHER PILE.

4. You may use all of one page or mix pages, if desired.

5. If you want larger cards or different words, use $3'' \times 5''$ or $4'' \times 6''$ index cards and felt pen.

3-29 SIMILES PARTNERSHIP

Number of Players: Entire class

Materials Needed: • TRITE SIMILES CARDS

How to Play: Divide the class into two groups. Give each member of one group a "beginning" of a simile. Give each member of the second group an "ending" of a simile. Turn students loose to find the beginnings and endings that fit together. (Since these are trite, overused similes, this happens rather rapidly.)

After finding their partners, each twosome writes out two or three original similes with the same beginning. Take turns around the room and have one member of the partnership read the trite simile and their partner read their original simile to the class. When everyone has had a chance, vote on the five best original similes, have students write them on the chalkboard, and discuss as a group why they are appealing. Emphasize that trite similes have lost most of their impact because of overuse.

3-30 SIMILES GAME

Number of Players: 2 to 5

How to Play: Using cards as prepared above, place face-down on the table the "beginning" and "ending" piles. In turn, each player draws two cards, one from each pile, not showing them to the other players. There are no discards.

During a turn the player lays face-up on the table any *completed* similes and reads them aloud. (Other players can challenge if they think the simile is incorrect. The teacher settles all challenges.) During a turn a player can demand a sight-unseen trade of a beginning or ending card with any other player. The player getting rid of all cards at a turn does not have to draw any new cards, and is the winner.

TRITE SIMILES USING <u>AS</u>

BUSY AS A	BEE	SMOOTH AS	SILK
WHITE AS	SNOW	BRIGHT AS A	PENNY
CLEAR AS A	BELL	CUTE AS A	BUTTON
STRONG AS AN	OX	LIGHT AS A	FEATHER
STUBBORN AS A	MULE	DEEP AS THE	OCEAN
GOOD AS	GOLD	COOL AS A	CUCUMBER
BOLD AS	BRASS	HAPPY AS A	LARK
HARD AS A	ROCK	SHARP AS A	TACK
LOOSE AS A	GOOSE	SLIPPERY AS AN	EEL
CLEAN AS A	WHISTLE	CURIOUS AS A	CAT
THIN AS A	RAIL	ROTTEN AS AN	APPLE
WARM AS	TOAST	PATIENT AS	JOB
SWEET AS	CANDY	SOFT AS	VELVET

MORE TRITE SIMILES USING As

BROWN AS A	BERRY	TOUGH AS	LEATHER
BLACK AS	COAL	BLIND AS A	BAT
PROUD AS A	PEACOCK	SLY AS A	FOX
CRAZY AS A	LOON	DRY AS A	BONE
STIFF AS A	BOARD	FIT AS A	FIDDLE
GREEN AS	GRASS	DEAD AS A	DOORNAIL
FLAT AS A	PANCAKE	HEAVY AS	LEAD
FAT AS A	PIG	SOUR AS A	LEMON
RICH AS	MIDAS	RED AS A	BEET
PLAYFUL AS A	KITTEN	SHY AS A	VIOLET
OLD AS	TIME	HUGE AS AN	ELEPHANT
HOT AS	HADES	PRETTY AS A	PICTURE
BRAVE AS A	LION	QUIET AS A	MOUSE

TRITE SIMILES USING LIKE

WADDLED LIKE A	DUCK	ATE LIKE A	PIG
WRINKLED LIKE A	PRUNE	CLEVER LIKE A	FOX
WORKED LIKE A	HORSE	LAUGHED LIKE A	HYENA
STIFF LIKE A	BOARD	EYES LIKE	SAUCERS
HANDLED IT LIKE A	PRO	SANK LIKE A	ROCK
PURRED LIKE A	KITTEN	SMELLED LIKE A	SKUNK
CRIED LIKE A	BABY	SANG LIKE A	CANARY
CHATTERED LIKE	MAGPIES	LOOKED LIKE AN	ANGEL
BLED LIKE A	STUCK PIG	RAN LIKE A	DEER
BURST LIKE A	BUBBLE	DROVE LIKE A	MANIAC
SWAM LIKE A	FISH	SMOKED LIKE A	CHIMNEY
STOOD LIKE A	STATUE	MEMORY LIKE AN	ELEPHANT
SHAPED LIKE A	PEAR	KICKED LIKE A	MULE

3-31   AUTHOR/TITLE

To the Teacher: Run off one AUTHOR/TITLE GAME BOARD for each group of four or fewer players. The game board consists of two pages attached in the middle (labeled left and right). Run off the 16 game cards on tagboard. Laminate, if possible. Emphasize that fiction books are grouped together alphabetically by author on the library shelves.

Players: 2 to 4

Materials Needed: • AUTHOR/TITLE GAME BOARD

  • AUTHOR/TITLE CARDS

  • 1 marker for each player

How to Play: Draw an author card. Name books or stories by the author. Turn the card over to see if you are correct. Put the card on the bottom of the pack. Advance the number of spaces that equals the number of books you named by that author. (Not every title is on the back of the card and authors are constantly writing, so if all players agree that the title you give is by that author, you may count it in the number of spaces you can move forward.) The first person to reach the center (GOAL) is the winner.

Rationale: It is hoped that by hearing old favorites over and over, the authors' names will stick in the students' minds. This game should help students find additional books by these famous authors more easily as they see the correct spellings of their names repeatedly while playing the game.

Modification: Updated cards with titles and authors you wish to have students learn can be added and/or substituted as desired.

AUTHOR/TITLE GAME BOARD (LEFT HALF)

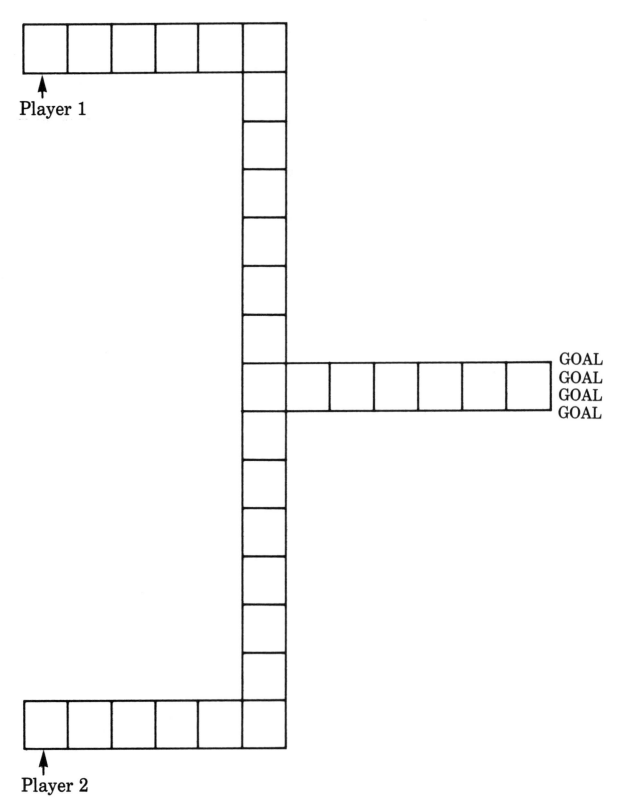

AUTHOR/TITLE GAME BOARD (RIGHT HALF)

Player 3

Player 4

AUTHOR/TITLE CARDS (FRONT)—1ST PAGE

ROALD DAHL	WILSON RAWLS
BEVERLY CLEARY	MARGUERITE HENRY
JUDY BLUME	JOSEPH KRUMGOLD
E. B. WHITE	JUDITH VIORST

AUTHOR/TITLE CARDS (BACK)—1ST PAGE

The BFG Charlie and the Chocolate Factory Danny, Champion of the World James and the Giant Peach The Enormous Crocodile The Magic Finger	Summer of the Monkeys Where the Red Fern Grows
Dear Mr. Henshaw Socks Ramona the Pest The Mouse and the Motorcycle Otis Spofford Ribsy Henry and Beezus Ralph S. Mouse	Justin Morgan Had a Horse King of the Wind Misty of Chincoteague Misty's Twilight
Superfudge Tales of a Fourth Grade Nothing The Green Kangaroo It's Not the End of the World Are You There, God? It's Me, Margaret Tiger Eyes Blubber	. . . And Now Miguel Onion John
Charlotte's Web Stuart Little Trumpet of the Swan	The Tenth Good Thing About Barney Sunday Morning

AUTHOR/TITLE CARDS (FRONT)—2ND PAGE

MADELEINE L'ENGLE	JAY WILLIAMS
BETSY BYARS	O. HENRY
ROBERT PECK	SCOTT O'DELL
WALTER FARLEY	ROBERT CORMIER

The Arm of the Starfish A Wrinkle in Time A Wind in the Door A Swiftly Tilting Planet	Danny Dunn (series) The City Witch and the Country Witch The Reward Worth Having Petronella The Magic Grandfather
Trouble River Cracker Jackson The Pinballs The Midnight Fox The T-V Kid After the Goatman	The Gift of the Magi The Ransom of Red Chief
Spanish Hoof A Day No Pigs Would Die Clunie Soup	Island of the Blue Dolphins The Black Pearl Sing Down the Moon Streams to the River, River to the Sea
The Black Stallion	I Am the Cheese The Chocolate War Beyond the Chocolate War After the First Death Eight Plus One: Stories

Section Four

SOCIAL STUDIES, SCIENCE, MATHEMATICS, AND THE ARTS

4-1   FAMOUS PLACES

Match these structures with the letter of their locations. Shade or color each letter box in the grid as you answer. The shaded shape is also an important place. What is it? _____

N	P	Y	J	Q	N	Z
U	W	E	P	L	S	V
O	B	R	W	X	A	O
K	I	Z	Q	R	H	M
V	F	N	T	S	D	N
W	C	O	V	Q	G	U

_____   1. Parthenon

_____   2. Pyramids

_____   3. Mayan Temple

_____   4. Temple of Heaven

_____   5. Taj Mahal

_____   6. Cologne Cathedral

_____   7. Astrodome

_____   8. Leaning Tower

_____   9. Eiffel Tower

_____ 10. Empire State Building

_____ 11. U.S. Capitol

_____ 12. St. Paul's Cathedral

_____ 13. Lunghwa Pagoda

A. Peking, China

B. New York City

C. Athens, Greece

D. Pisa, Italy

E. Houston, Texas

F. Paris, France

G. Giza, Egypt

H. Washington, D.C.

I. London, England

J. Yucatan

K. Shanghai, China

L. Cologne, Germany

M. Agra, India

4-2   ALPHA CHALLENGE

Most everyone can put words into alphabetical order by the first letter. These capitals of states of the United States provide a bigger challenge. Can you arrange each group in proper alpha order? Remember, if the first letter is the same, you will have to go to the second or third letter or even beyond!

Hint: Alphabetize <u>St.</u> as if it were spelled out (<u>Saint</u>).

Group I

Atlanta (Georgia)
Augusta (Maine)
Annapolis (Maryland)
Albany (New York)
Austin (Texas)

Group II

Sacramento (California)
Springfield (Illinois)
St. Paul (Minnesota)
Santa Fe (New Mexico)
Salem (Oregon)
Salt Lake City (Utah)

Group III

Boise (Idaho)
Baton Rouge (Louisiana)
Boston (Massachusetts)
Bismarck (North Dakota)

Group IV

Carson City (Nevada)
Concord (New Hampshire)
Columbus (Ohio)
Columbia (South Dakota)
Charleston (West Virginia)
Cheyenne (Wyoming)

Group I

_____

_____

_____

_____

_____

Group III

_____

_____

_____

_____

Group II

_____

_____

_____

_____

_____

_____

Group IV

_____

_____

_____

_____

_____

_____

4-3   CAPITAL FUN

Take syllables from the CAPITALS SYLLABANK and put them together to spell the capitals of the states indicated. It is a good idea to cross out each of the 65 syllables as you use it.

1. Alabama   __ __ __ __   __ __ __   __ __   __

2. Alaska   __ __   __ __ __ __

3. Arizona   __ __ __ __   __ __ __

4. Colorado   __ __ __   __ __

5. Connecticut   __ __ __ __   __ __ __ __

6. Florida   __ __ __   __ __ __   __ __ __   __ __ __

7. Hawaii   __ __ __   __   __ __   __ __

8. Indiana   __ __   __ __ __   __ __   __ __   __
                    __ __ __

9. Iowa   __ __ __   __ __ __ __ __

10. Kansas   __ __   __ __   __ __

11. Kentucky   __ __ __ __ __   __ __ __ __

12. Michigan   __ __ __   __ __ __

13. Mississippi   __ __ __ __   __ __ __

14. Nebraska   __ __ __   __ __ __ __

15. New Jersey   __ __ __ __   __ __ __

16. N. Carolina   __ __   __ __ __ __

17. Pennsylvania   __ __ __ __   __ __ __ __ __ __

18. Rhode Island   __ __ __ __   __ __ __ __ __ __

19. S. Dakota   __ __   __ __ __ __

20. Tennessee   __ __ __ __   __ __ __ __ __

21. Vermont   __ __ __ __   __ __ __ __

22. Virginia   __ __ __ __   __ __ __ __

23. Washington   __   __ __ __ __ __ __

24. Wisconsin   __ __ __   __   __ __ __

147

4-3

CAPITAL FUN
(Cont'd)

CAPITALS SYLLABANK

A   AN   AP   BURG   COLN   DEN   DENCE

DES   DI   ER   ERRE   FORD   FORT   FRANK

GOM   HAR   HART   HAS   HOV   I   I

IER   IN   JACK   JU   KA   LAN   LA   LEIGH

LIN   LIS   LU   LU   LYM   MAD   MOINES

MOND   MONT   MONT   NASH   NEAU

NIX   O   O   O   PE   PEL   PHOE   PI

PI   PROV   RA   RICH   RIS   SEE   SING

SON   SON   TAL   TO   TON   TREN   VER

VILLE   Y

Name _____

4-4   # CITIES AROUND THE WORLD

Across

2. Istanbul
3. Taipei
5. Tokyo
8. Baghdad
9. Buenos Aires
12. Mexico City
14. Moscow
16. Sydney
17. Paris

Down

1. Rio de Janeiro
2. Bangkok
4. Calcutta
6. Shanghai
7. New York
10. Lisbon
11. Berlin
13. Rome
15. Madrid

COUNTRIES OF THE WORLD

Turkey	Spain	China	Mexico	France	Argentina
Japan	Russia	Germany	Italy	United States	India
Taiwan	Thailand	Iran	Australia	Portugal	Brazil

4-5 ROUNDABOUTS

The object of a roundabout is to find the hidden word. The first three are the easiest, the next three a little harder, and the last three the most difficult. Follow the instructions for each set of three.

Set 1: Start with any letter. Go around in one direction and spell out the correct word. **Hint:** States.

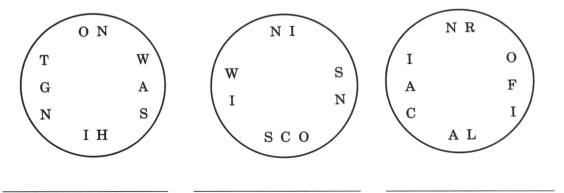

_____ _____ _____

Set 2: Start with any letter. Go around in one direction and end with the center letter to spell out the correct word. **Hint:** Places.

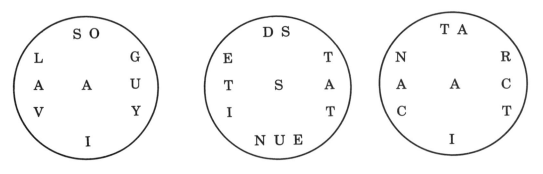

_____ _____ _____

Set 3: Start with any letter. Go around in one direction and end with the center letter to spell out the correct word. **Hint:** Occupations.

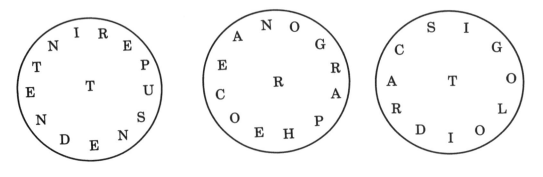

_____ _____ _____

Name _____

4-6   A STATE BY ANY OTHER NAME

Every state has a name, but it also has a nickname. The nickname is often found on the license plate of the state. Can you match them by crossing out the extra letters in the state? The letters are in order. The states will be in alphabetical order. Be sure to capitalize the first letter of each state!

1. ablcadsekfa   _____   The Last Frontier

2. brarkcacniseas   _____   Land of Opportunity

3. fcoilcorlaydio   _____   Centennial State

4. ehpawuaiir   _____   Aloha State

5. wiplluinvocis   _____   Prairie State

6. riobrwba   _____   Hawkeye State

7. elovuxizsirapna   _____   Pelican State

8. nmpirssoisswippei   _____   Magnolia State

9. mgosntlanra   _____   Treasure State

10. antew hmampvshoicre   _____   Granite State

11. nazenw smoexpicto   _____   Land of Enchantment

12. notrtjh dmapkowtra   _____   Peace Garden State

13. poukelmahwovmqa   _____   Sooner State

14. petnniskymlivwanpica   _____   Keystone State

15. etawennetspsee   _____   Volunteer State

16. cuewtaph   _____   Beehive State

17. zvnirhgoicnipa   _____   Old Dominion

18. mwoasphibntgtpown   _____   Evergreen State

19. awimspcionrspien   _____   Badger State

20. bwoyeomninjg   _____   Equality State

4-7   **NAME THAT STATE**

Across

5. Sunshine State
8. Grand Canyon State
10. Hawkeye State
11. Beaver State
13. Hoosier State
14. Sunflower State
15. Garden State

Down

1. Gem State
2. Golden State
3. Lone Star State
4. Green Mountain State
6. Buckeye State
7. Cornhusker State
9. Empire State
12. Pine Tree State

NAME THAT STATE				
Vermont	New Jersey	New York	Iowa	Florida
Nebraska	Idaho	Indiana	Kansas	Maine
California	Oregon	Ohio	Texas	Arizona

4-8 HAVING FUN WITH STATE ABBREVIATIONS (I)

Combine the abbreviations for the states below to form words.

1. Alabama + Mississippi			
2. Arkansas + Idaho			
3. California + Indiana			
4. Colorado + Delaware			
5. Delaware + Alabama			
6. Florida + Alaska			
7. Georgia + Indiana			
8. Hawaii + Delaware			
9. Indiana + California			
10. Louisiana + Delaware			
11. Maine + Alabama			
12. Massachusetts + Idaho			
13. Michigan + Maine			
14. Missouri + Mississippi			
15. Nebraska + Arkansas			
16. Oregon + Alabama			
17. Pennsylvania + Illinois			
18. Rhode Island + North Dakota			
19. South Carolina + Arkansas			
20. Virginia + Indiana			
21. Washington + Delaware			
22. Wisconsin + Nebraska			
23. Wisconsin + North Dakota			

4-9 HAVING FUN WITH STATE ABBREVIATIONS (II)

Combine the abbreviations for the states below to form words.

1. Alabama + Arkansas

2. Arkansas + Iowa

3. California + Maine

4. Colorado + Illinois

5. Delaware + Arkansas

6. Georgia + Louisiana

7. Georgia + Maine

8. Louisiana + Idaho

9. Louisiana + Indiana

10. Maine + Georgia

11. Massachusetts + Nebraska

12. Michigan + California

13. Missouri + Delaware

14. Pennsylvania + Idaho

15. Pennsylvania + Indiana

16. Pennsylvania + Nebraska

17. Rhode Island + Maine

18. Rhode Island + Mississippi

19. Virginia + Nebraska

20. Washington + Illinois

21. Washington + Nebraska

22. Washington + North Dakota

23. Wisconsin + Delaware

4-10 HAVING FUN WITH STATE ABBREVIATIONS (III)

Combine the abbreviations for the states below to form words.

1. Arkansas + Kansas

2. Arkansas + Mississippi

3. California + Mississippi

4. California + Nebraska

5. Colorado + Alabama

6. Colorado + Indiana

7. Colorado + Louisiana

8. Colorado + Maine

9. Colorado + Massachusetts

10. Colorado + Nebraska

11. Delaware + Michigan

12. Delaware + Missouri

13. Georgia + Mississippi

14. Louisiana + Maine

15. Louisiana + Nebraska

16. Louisiana + Virginia

17. Maine + Missouri

18. Maine + North Dakota

19. Massachusetts + Delaware

20. Massachusetts + Illinois

21. Massachusetts + Indiana

22. Michigan + Nebraska

23. Rhode Island + Delaware

4-11   CUT-OFF COMMUNICATION

See if you can join the words or letters that have been cut off. Restore communication again! Connect communication methods with lines (without crossing any other lines). List methods on the lines below. Watch spelling!

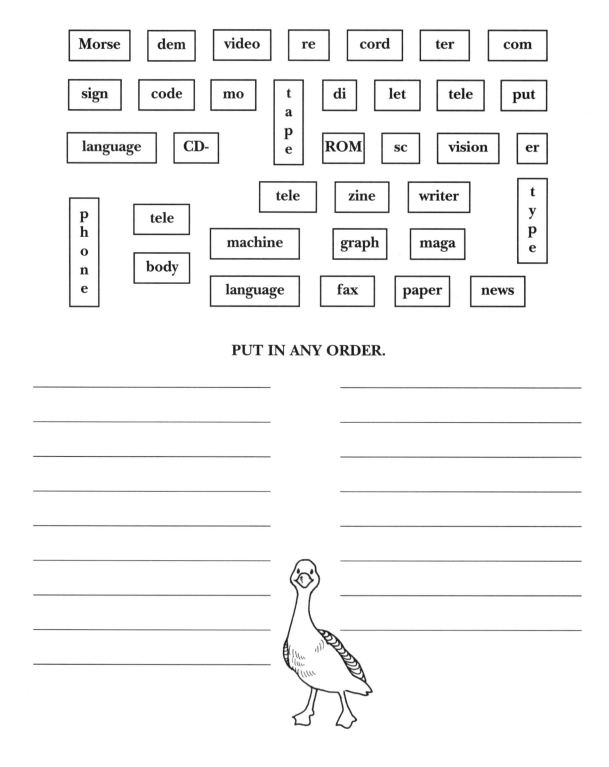

Morse	dem	video	re	cord	ter	com
sign	code	mo	t a p e	di	let	tele	put
language	CD-		ROM	sc	vision	er

tele   zine   writer

p h o n e   tele   body   machine   graph   maga   t y p e

language   fax   paper   news

PUT IN ANY ORDER.

_____   _____

_____   _____

_____   _____

_____   _____

_____   _____

_____   _____

_____

© 1996 by The Center for Applied Research in Education

Name _____

4-12   GETTING THERE IS HALF THE FUN

Observe the squares corresponding to the numbers and letters listed. If a form of transportation (no matter how silly) is listed, color in any parts of those squares. Leave blank any squares that do not correspond with forms of transportation.

When you finish, follow the three directions at the bottom of the page. You should end up with a picture of a form of transportation that shows that getting there is half the fun.

a	b	a	b	a	b	a	b	a	b	a	b
25		26		27		28		29		30	
c	d	c	d	c	d	c	d	c	d	c	d
a	b	a	b	a	b	a	b	a	b	a	b
19		20		21		22		23		24	
c	d	c	d	c	d	c	d	c	d	c	d
a	b	a	b	a	b	a	b	a	b	a	b
13		14		15		16		17		18	
c	d	c	d	c	d	c	d	c	d	c	d
a	b	a	b	a	b	a	b	a	b	a	b
7		8		9		10		11		12	
c	d	c	d	c	d	c	d	c	d	c	d
a	b	a	b	a	b	a	b	a	b	a	b
1		2		3		4		5		6	
c	d	c	d	c	d	c	d	c	d	c	d

1a. telephone
 b. computer
 c. television
 d. Morse code
2a. automobile
 b. helicopter
 c. newspaper
 d. horse
3a. motorcycle
 b. bicycle
 c. skateboard
 d. ship
4a. locomotive
 b. submarine
 c. surfboard
 d. snowmobile

5a. snowshoes
 b. roller blades
 c. ice skates
 d. magazine
6a. letter
 b. typewriter
 c. telegraph
 d. radio
7a. factory
 b. fax
 c. school
 d. airplane
8a. book
 b. CD-ROM
 c. bus
 d. taxi

9a. video player
 b. record player
 c. escalator
 d. elevator
10a. dishwasher
 b. microwave
 c. wheelchair
 d. cable car
11a. copy machine
 b. sign language
 c. truck
 d. stilts
12a. modem
 b. movie
 c. moped
 d. disc

Directions:

1. Draw a line from center of square 7 to center of square 27.
2. Draw a line from center of square 12 to center of square 27.
3. Draw a line from center of square 9 to center of square 27.

157

4-13   JOB-RELATED NAMES

Many last names came into being because of the job the person had. These interesting names have been handed down over the generations and still exist today. See how many you can list.

Example: Shepherd

_____   _____

_____   _____

_____   _____

_____   _____

_____   _____

_____   _____

_____   _____

_____   _____

_____   _____

_____   _____

_____   _____

Name _____

4-14   BUILD A CAREER

Build the letter blocks into proper sequence to find careers. Write the careers on the lines.

1. | ea | er | pr | ch | _____

2. | li | ce | po | _____

3. | ma | re | fi | n | _____

4. | er | of | ro | _____

5. | rb | ba | er | _____

6. | er | wy | la | _____

7. | ct | or | do | _____

8. | ch | me | ic | an | _____

9. | er | gr | oc | _____

10. | st | ug | dr | gi | _____

11. | it | ss | re | wa | _____

12. | r | he | tc | bu | _____

13. | si | er | ng | _____

14. | er | cl | k | _____

Name _____

4-15   FLAG IDENTIFICATION

Most Americans can readily identify the flag of the United States with its thirteen red and white stripes representing the original colonies and its 50 white stars on a blue background representing each of the 50 states. The flags of other countries also have symbolic meanings. Many are quite easily recognized.

How many flags can you match with the country they represent? Choose countries from the WORLD BANK and put them on the blanks.

Hint: If you need help, an almanac is a great resource!

1. red circle on white   _____

2. white star on blue   _____

3. white cross on red   _____

4. blue, white, red vertical stripes   _____

5. green, white, red vertical stripes   _____

6. red, yellow, green vertical stripes with <u>R</u> in middle   _____

7. red, white, blue horizontal stripes with insignia in middle   _____

8. solid green   _____

9. yellow star in middle on red   _____

10. red, white, red vertical patches with red maple leaf   _____

WORLD BANK

Canada	Rwanda
France	Switzerland
Italy	Somalia
Japan	South Africa
Libya	Vietnam

4-16   PRESIDENTS

Name	Born	Age Died	Name	Born	Age Died
George Washington	VA	67	Grover Cleveland	NJ	71
John Adams	MA	90	Benjamin Harrison	OH	67
Thomas Jefferson	VA	83	Grover Cleveland	NJ	71
James Madison	VA	85	William McKinley	OH	58
James Monroe	VA	73	Theodore Roosevelt	NY	60
John Quincy Adams	MA	80	William Howard Taft	OH	72
Andrew Jackson	SC	78	Woodrow Wilson	VA	67
Martin Van Buren	NY	79	Warren Harding	OH	57
William Harrison	VA	68	Calvin Coolidge	VT	60
John Tyler	VA	71	Herbert Hoover	LA	90
James Polk	NC	53	Franklin Roosevelt	NY	63
Zachary Taylor	VA	65	Harry S. Truman	MO	88
Millard Filmore	NY	74	Dwight Eisenhower	TX	78
Franklin Pierce	NH	64	John F. Kennedy	MA	46
James Buchanan	PA	77	Lyndon B. Johnson	TX	64
Abraham Lincoln	KY	56	Richard Nixon	CA	81
Andrew Johnson	NC	66	Gerald R. Ford	NE	—
Ulysses S. Grant	OH	63	James Earl Carter	GA	—
Rutherford B. Hayes	OH	70	Ronald Reagan	IL	—
James Garfield	OH	49	George Bush	MA	—
Chester Arthur	VT	57	William Clinton	AR	—

1. How many presidents were over 80 when they died? _____

2. How many DIFFERENT presidents were named James? _____

3. How many DIFFERENT presidents' last names began with <u>C?</u> _____

4. What president died the youngest? _____

5. How many presidents were born in Virginia? _____

6. How many presidents were born in Ohio? _____

7. Who was our 16th president? _____

8. Who was our 32nd president? _____

9. Who was our president in 1995? _____

4-17   SECRET ANIMAL JUMBLE

Unscramble the jumbled letters to reveal the names of seven different animals. Then you will be able to find the secret animal by putting the circled letters on the lines below.

1.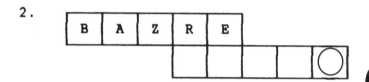

M A C L E

2.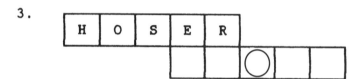

B A Z R E

3.

H O S E R

4.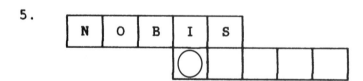

G R I T E

5.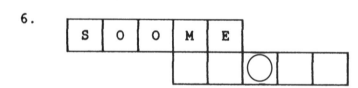

N O B I S

6.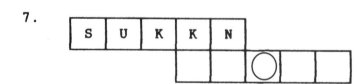

S O O M E

7.

S U K K N

SECRET ANIMAL (like a reindeer): ____ ____ ____ ____ ____ ____ ____
                                    1   2   3   4   5   6   7

4-18   CHEWING THE CUD

These animals are called ruminants because they are all cud-chewing. The word <u>ruminate</u> means to chew over or mull over and comes from the same root.

Some of these animals are probably familiar; others may be new to you. Figure out how many syllables each has and color or shade one box for each syllable. Then add the number of shaded boxes in each column. If the two totals match, you probably have figured out the syllables correctly.

1. giraffe   ☐☐☐
2. zebu   ☐☐☐
3. buffalo   ☐☐☐
4. ox   ☐☐☐
5. addax   ☐☐☐
6. camel   ☐☐☐
7. impala   ☐☐☐
8. gnu   ☐☐☐
9. goat   ☐☐☐
10. eland   ☐☐☐

11. deer   ☐☐☐
12. gazelle   ☐☐☐
13. yak   ☐☐☐
14. bongo   ☐☐☐
15. oryx   ☐☐☐
16. caribou   ☐☐☐
17. ibex   ☐☐☐
18. moose   ☐☐☐
19. kudu   ☐☐☐
20. wapiti   ☐☐☐

Add the total syllables in the first column. Put your answer on the line below.

Add the total syllables in the second column. Put your answer on the line below.

_____

_____

163

4-19   THE MALE OF THE SPECIES

Often the name of a male animal is different from the general name of the species; sometimes it is the same. Put each male of the species in his proper place by using the word configuration clues (shape of letters above and below the line).

Example: elephant

1. fox

2. seal

3. goat

4. donkey

5. deer

6. horse

7. hog

Name _____

4-20   WILD CATS

Fill in the missing letters. Use the WORD JUNGLE to help you. Then take a letter from each column to get good advice about these wild cats.

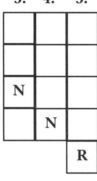
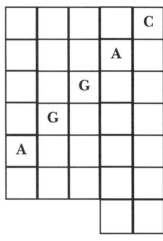

1. 2.   **3. 4. 5.**   **6. 7. 8. 9. 10.**

Advice:

WORD JUNGLE

BOBCAT		JAGUAR		LEOPARD
LYNX	LION	COUGAR		CARACAL
OCELOT		TIGER		CHEETAH

165

4-21   GOING TO THE DOGS

Look in the DOG POUND to find the dogs that answer the following puzzles.

DOG POUND

Collie	Basenji	Great Dane	Chihuahua
Dachshund	Pekinese	Lhasa Apso	Dalmatian
Setter	Griffon	Papillon	Husky
Pointer	Retriever	Pinscher	Saint Bernard
Hound	Spaniel	Pomeranian	Rottweiler
Terrier	Malamute	Poodle	Mastiff
Schnauzer	Sheepdog	Bulldog	Keeshonden
Beagle	German Shepherd	Chow Chow	Samoyede

List the dogs beginning with the letter <u>D:</u>

_____   _____

List the dogs having two syllables:

_____   _____   _____   _____

_____   _____   _____   _____

_____   _____   _____   _____

_____   _____

List the dog that rhymes with <u>muskie:</u> _____

List the dog that backwards is <u>nollipap:</u> _____

List the dogs that have the last two syllables repeated:

_____   _____

© 1996 by The Center for Applied Research in Education

4-22 SECRET BIRD JUMBLE

Unscramble the jumbled letters to reveal the names of six different birds. If you solve the puzzle correctly, you will be able to find the secret bird by putting the circled letters on the lines below.

1.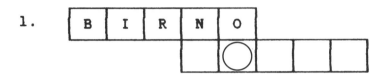

2.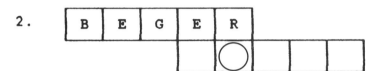

3.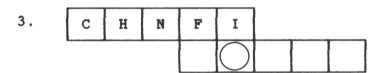

4.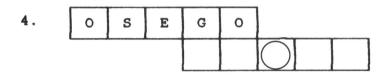

5.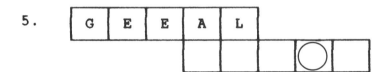

6.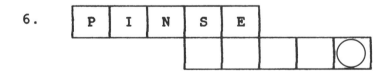

SECRET BIRD (Maryland's State Bird): ___ ___ ___ ___ ___ ___
                                     1   2   3   4   5   6

4-23 BIRD-O-GRAM

Use the scrambled letters to form the longest words you can. You may leave letters out if you can't think of a 6-letter word. Your points will be the numbers shown on each letter tile.

Hint: Each word can be made into a 6-letter bird. If you can figure out the birds, you will probably have the best score (54).

1.

| B 3 | E 1 | P 3 | H 4 | O 1 | E 1 |

_____ Points

2.

| F 4 | O 1 | N 1 | C 3 | A 1 | L 1 |

_____ Points

3.

| S 1 | H 4 | R 1 | U 1 | T 1 | H 4 |

_____ Points

4.

| S 1 | R 1 | E 1 | G 2 | O 1 | U 1 |

_____ Points

5.

| P 3 | I 1 | G 2 | M 3 | A 1 | E 1 |

_____ Points

_____ **TOTAL**

4-24   BIRD COLORS

These birds and fowls all have a color in their name. Color in the boxes to show you know the names of the birds. Some of the boxes COULD have more than one correct answer, but if you cross out the colors in the BIRD COLOR CHOICES as you go, you will use them all with none left over.

Hint: Do the ones you're sure of first.

1. [ ] DUCK

2. [ ] GOOSE

3. BOB [ ]

4. [ ] -HEADED WOODPECKER

5. [ ] -BELLIED SAPSUCKER

6. [ ] MARTIN

7. [ ] JAY

8. [ ] BIRD

9. [ ] TANAGER

10. [ ] -WINGED BLACKBIRD

What color am I?

BIRD COLOR CHOICES

Red/Red/Scarlet/Black/Black/Purple/Blue/Blue/Yellow/White

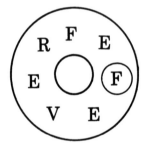

4-25   PLANT RINGS

Begin with the circled letters and go clockwise or counterclockwise to form the names of common plants. Spell the name of each plant on the line below the ring.

You must supply the missing last letter and put it in the circle in the middle. These circled last letters, when put together, will give you a secret message to put at the bottom of the page.

1.
     N A T
     R   I
     A (C) O

_____

2.
     W I N
     I   K
        L
     R E (P)

_____

3.
     (G) I
     A   N
        E
     R D

_____

4.
     I
     O   (V)
     L   E

_____

5.
     R F E
     E   (F)
     V E

_____

6.
     D A
     (A)   C
     V O

_____

7.
     (P)
     E   E
     P   P

_____

8.
     (P) C A
     I   B
     G G Y

_____

LAST LETTERS: ___ ___ ___ ___   ___ ___ ___ ___

4-26 POISONOUS PLANTS

Some species of these plants lead a double life. They are beautiful, but also poisonous. In certain instances the leaves are poisonous; in other cases the berries or flowers are the culprit. You should take care when handling any of these plants!

Some of the letters in these plants also lead a double life. Sometimes two different letters make only one sound, either because the sounds are combined or one of the letters is silent. First, circle any two DIFFERENT letters from the list where two letters make only one sound. (Don't count e's.) Write these letters on the lines. Then, underline any two of the SAME letters that are DOUBLED (vowels or consonants). Write them on the lines provided.

1. aconite
2. belladonna
3. bittersweet
4. castor-oil
5. delphinium
6. digitalis
7. fennel
8. hellebore
9. hemlock
10. henbane
11. holly
12. ivy

13. jimson
14. laurel
15. locoweed
16. mandrake
17. mushroom
18. nettle
19. oleander
20. parsnip
21. pokeweed
22. primrose
23. rhubarb
24. sumac

TWO DIFFERENT LETTERS MAKING ONE SOUND (not counting e's):

1. _____   2. _____   3. _____   4. _____   5. _____   6. _____

TWO OF THE SAME LETTERS DOUBLED (count vowels and consonants):

7. _____   8. _____   9. _____   10. _____   11. _____   12. _____

13. _____   14. _____   15. _____   16. _____   17. _____

4-27   **FRUIT LOOPS**

See if you can loop 16 fruits. You will need to figure out the missing vowels (a, e, i, o, u) and put them on the lines. Names of fruits will only go left to right or top to bottom.

```
L __ M __ N C B __ P R __ C O T X R T
W R B P G D __ Z __ C N B M __ P L K
G R __ P E W R T N G F L G N V X Z
Y D N H J K __ C __ Q P F __ G F R E
P __ __ C H W N P __ V C C H __ R R Y
S J N B M N G W P L __ M N R P T T
Q Y __ P P L __ D P C B T L __ M __ W
T R Y G H S C B L P L M B N V F H
R __ __ S __ N X P __ __ R B M __ L __ N
```

Across

_____

_____

_____

_____

_____

Down

_____

_____

_____

_____

_____

_____

_____

_____

_____

© 1996 by The Center for Applied Research in Education

Name _____

LET'S GO ANGLING

You have to go angling to get these freshwater fish! Every fish in the word search changes directions in the middle of the stream.

Example: s
  h
  i n e r

Use the FISH POND to remind you of some freshwater fish you may have forgotten about. Then put a net (loop) around each and every one.

A	B	N	C	H	C	D	M	E	F	G	C	S	G
H	E	R	I	B	R	E	A	J	B	A	S	A	H
T	A	K	L	L	S	U	N	T	T	O	M	N	N
P	P	I	E	U	U	O	P	F	R	Q	W	R	A
L	L	I	G	E	C	I	S	C	I	O	H	F	R
S	T	P	I	K	A	U	V	O	W	S	U	N	I
X	Y	E	E	E	Z	R	P	A	T	B	H	T	P
C	D	R	C	H	L	E	F	U	R	G	E	O	N

FISH POND

			sturgeon
bass	carp	eel	sucker
bluegill	catfish	perch	sunfish
bowfin	cisco	pike	tench
bream	crappie	piranha	trout

173

4-29   SOMETHING BUGGING YOU?

Is something bugging you? Maybe it's just one of these fellows!

Begin with the upper left letter in each box and follow the letters clockwise to find out what it might be. The number in the center of each box will tell you which letter to put on the line at the bottom of the page. When you unscramble these letters and write the word in the boxes, MAYBE you'll have what you need to get rid of what's bugging you!

C	R	I
	7	C
T	E	K

F	I	R
	5	E
Y	L	F

L	A	D
	2	Y
G	U	B

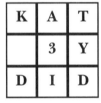

1. _____   2. _____   3. _____

K	A	T
	3	Y
D	I	D

T	E	R
	3	M
E	T	I

M	E	A
G	4	L
U	B	Y

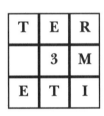

4. _____   5. _____   6. _____

G	A	L
P	5	L
S	A	W

S	T	I
G	1	N
U	B	K

H	O	N
E	7	E
E	B	Y

H	O	U
Y	8	S
L	F	E

7. _____   8. _____   9. _____   10. _____

Scrambled word: _____

What you need: ▢▢▢ ▢▢▢▢▢▢

4-30

ANATOMY

Just as many parts of our anatomy function so silently that we are unaware of them, some letters function silently in words. Put a slash through any silent letters in these internal organs of the human body.

1. b r a i n
2. l a r y n x
3. t r a c h e a
4. l u n g
5. h e a r t
6. s p l e e n
7. l i v e r
8. k i d n e y
9. s t o m a c h
10. i n t e s t i n e
11. p a n c r e a s
12. g a l l b l a d d e r

Find the four-letter words hidden inside these internal organs. Put them in the puzzle below.

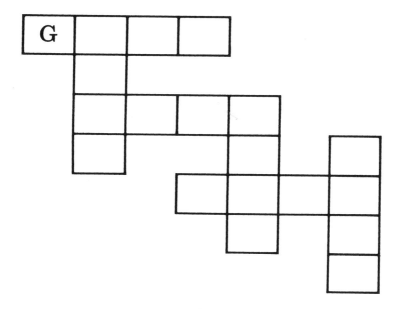

4-31   **JEWELS AND GEMS**

These gems were at the jewelry counter in alphabetical order. Several customers were only interested in green stones, though, so the store manager decided to group them by color.

Figure out the codes to see which gems the manager put in each color group. Write the names of the gems on the correct lines.

Names of Gems	Stock Code Numbers
amethyst	101PL
amber	102Y
aquamarine	103B
bloodstone	104G
carnelian	105R
citrine	106Y
diamond	107CL
emerald	108G
garnet	109R
jade	110G
lapis lazuli	111B
moonstone	112W
olivine	113G
onyx	114BL
pearl	115W
peridot	116G
ruby	117R
sapphire	118B
topaz	119Y
turquoise	120B

Green

1. _____
2. _____
3. _____
4. _____
5. _____

Red

1. _____
2. _____
3. _____

Yellow

1. _____
2. _____
3. _____

White

1. _____
2. _____

Blue

1. _____
2. _____
3. _____
4. _____

Miscellaneous

1. _____
2. _____
3. _____

4-32 ORES AND MINERALS

The following ores and minerals are listed in alphabetical order. Reorder them according to the number of syllables each has. Place them under the proper category.

barite

bismuth

calcite

coal

copper

corundum

galena

gold

gypsum

hematite

lazulite

lignite

magnetite

platinum

pyrite

quartz

silver

stibnite

sulfur

talc

One Syllable

_____

_____

_____

_____

Two Syllables

_____

_____

_____

_____

_____

_____

_____

_____

_____

_____

Three Syllables

_____

_____

_____

_____

_____

_____

4-33   PROGRESSIONS

These sequences are in a logical order. Figure out what would come next. Put your answers on the lines.

1.  _____

2.   _____

3. Qp Ts Wv _____

4.  _____

5.  _____

6. 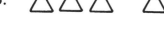 _____

7.  _____

8.  _____

_____

9.

10. AC BD F _____

4-34   ZIGZAG MATH SEARCH

Loop the math words in the word search puzzle. The catch is that you must make ONE zigzag or bend in each word.

Hint: W is often the stopper letter that tells you to zigzag. W is not used in any of the words. One word has been done to get you started.

```
A V E R W X I S D E C W W E M G E S W W W P R O
W P A R A W W E W W W I N F I W W W P W W E H B
W W R W L G W L W W W T M W R N W W W H G W O A
W O W W L W E P C W C N W A W A I N T E W W M B
O P Y H E X A M E W O W C Y L W C T W R W B W I
T W E L L I G W N I N W R W W I W T Y E U W W L
E W P R O P O R T E M E T E R W N W I S V A W I
N U R E G S N W W W D W W Q W W W D W O N L W T
U G W T R E M A I N W W W W U W H Y P E W W U W Y
S I W E A W W W W W W W W W A W T W W W R E W W
E F W W M W W W W W W N O I T W W R W C U B W W W
W W W W W W W W W W W W W W W W W A P E Z O I D
W W W W W W W W W W W W W W W W W W W W W W L W
W W W W W W W W W W W W W W W W W W W W W W W A
```

~~average~~	figure	proportion
axis	fraction	ratio
centimeter	hexagon	remainder
cone	hyperbola	rhombus
cube	hypotenuse	root
cylinder	infinity	segment
decimal	integer	sphere
ellipse	meter	trapezoid
equation	parallelogram	value
example	probability	

Name _____

4-35   MATH VOCABULARY SYMBOLS

Sometimes vocabulary words take the form of symbols. The symbols are used in place of words. Use the MATH SYMBOL BANK and your basic math knowledge to help you circle whether the items below are true (T) or false (F). When finished, use the statement (in symbols) at the bottom of the page to see how well you did.

1. $1 + 1 = 2$ T   F

2. $1 - 1 = 0$ T   F

3. $1 \times 1 = 2$ T   F

4. $1 \div 1 = 0$ T   F

5. $2 + 1 = 3 + 0$ T   F

6. $3 + 2 \neq 3 \times 2$ T   F

7. $5 = 5$ T   F

8. $10 < 9$ T   F

9. $9 > 7$ T   F

10. $8 \leqq 7 - 1$ T   F

11. $10 \geqq 7 + 3$ T   F

12. $\sqrt{4} = 2$ T   F

MATH SYMBOL BANK

+ plus	= is equal to	$\overset{=}{<}$ is equal to or less than
− minus	≠ is not equal to	$\overset{=}{>}$ is equal to or more than
× times	< is less than	
÷ divided by	> is more than	$\sqrt{}$ is the square root of

Statement: # T − # F = 4.

4-36 MATH VOCABULARY MUDDLE

The words in this muddle are basic mathematics operations, terms, and shapes. Letters connected by lines are the same. Use the MATH VOCABULARY BANK and lines to help you solve the muddle.

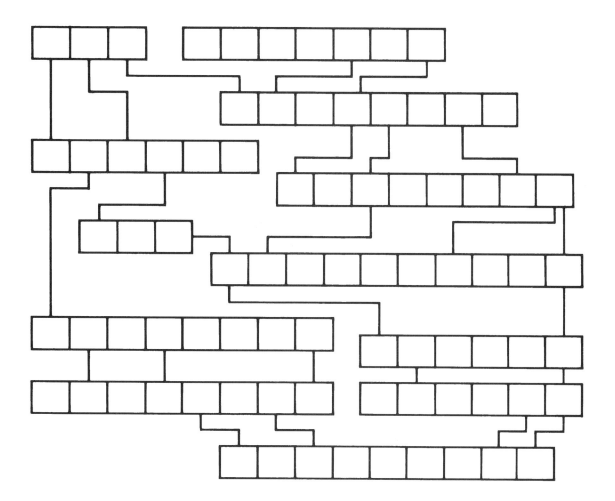

MATH VOCABULARY BANK

ADD	SUM	CIRCLE
SUBTRACT	DIFFERENCE	SQUARE
MULTIPLY	PRODUCT	TRIANGLE
DIVIDE	QUOTIENT	RECTANGLE

4-37   MONTH MATH

Use the <u>numbers of letters</u> in the months to solve these word/math puzzles.

1. Month with most letters: _____

   (number of letters): _____

  Month with least letters: _____

   (number of letters): _____

  Most letters plus least letters equals number of months in the year.

     _____ + _____ = _____

2. Three months with same number of letters:

  _____   _____   _____

  Number of letters in each: _____

  Number of months in year: _____

  Three times numbers of letters in each (above) equals two times number of months in year.

     3 × _____ = 2 × _____

     _____ = _____

3. June plus July plus 2 equals March plus April.

     _____ + _____ + 2 = _____ + _____

     _____ = _____

4. January times October equals September plus 40.

     _____ × _____ = _____ + 40

     _____ = _____

5. July times August equals November times May.

     _____ × _____ = _____ × _____

     _____ = _____

© 1996 by The Center for Applied Research in Education

4-38   MATH SQUARES

Figure out the correct numbers and fill in the blank squares. Use the NUMBER BANK below each puzzle to help you.

#1.

4	+		÷		= 3
+	/////	−	/////	x	/////
	x		+		= 6
−	/////	x	/////	÷	/////
	x		−		= 1
= 6	/////	= 8	/////	= 2	/////

NUMBER BANK: 1   2   2   2   3   3   4   5

#2.

16	+		÷		= 4
+	/////	x	/////	−	/////
	÷		x		= 2
÷	/////	−	/////	x	/////
	+		÷		= 1
= 6	/////	= 7	/////	= 12	/////

NUMBER BANK: 1   2   2   2   3   4   4   5

183

4-39   CAN YOU MAKE CENTS?

Answer the first six questions to be sure you know what these words mean. Then see if you can "make cents" in the last four situations. Cross out answers in the ANSWER BOX as you use them.

HOW MANY CENTS ARE THESE?

1. How much is a penny?   _____ cent

2. How much is a nickel?   _____ cents

3. How much is a dime?   _____ cents

4. How much is a quarter?   _____ cents

5. How much is a half-dollar?   _____ cents

6. How much is a dollar?   _____ cents

7. You give me a dime. I give you a nickel. How much do <u>you</u> have? _____

8. You give me a quarter and a penny. I give you a nickel and a dime. How much do <u>I</u> have? _____

9. I give you a dollar. You give me a half-dollar and a quarter. How much do <u>you</u> have? _____

10. I give you two quarters, a nickel, and a dime. You give me a half-dollar, two nickels, and five pennies. How much do <u>you</u> have? _____

11. How much do <u>I</u> have? _____

ANSWER BOX

0	1	5
5	10	11
25	25	50
65	100	

4-40   NUMBERS COUNT

Fill in the blanks with a number answer. Then total #1 through 6 and #7 through 12. You should get the same answer as #15.

1. _____ gun salute

2. lucky _____

3. _____ commandments

4. _____ inches to a foot

5. _____ days in a fortnight

6. _____ eggs in a dozen

7. _____ degrees Fahrenheit is freezing

8. unlucky _____

9. _____ total of highest numbers on pair of dice

10. _____ sides to an octagon

11. high _____

12. sing a song of _____ pence

13. Add answers to #1 through 6: _____

14. Add answers to #7 through 12: _____

15. _____ trombones (song)

Do #13 and #14 agree with #15? Then <u>YOU</u> are CORRECTOMUNDO!

4-41   HOW DO YOU MEASURE UP?

Every industry has a different way of measuring items. If you saw these measurements and sizes, would you recognize what they meant? Put the letters of the correct matches on the lines.

1. _____ 2 × 4   A. temperature

2. _____ 21 jewels   B. fuse

3. _____ 6-1/2 B   C. film

4. _____ 60 watt   D. clothes (baby)

5. _____ 6.70–15   E. clothes (female)

6. _____ 30 amps   F. rifle

7. _____ 35 mm   G. computer memory

8. _____ 30-06   H. shirt (male)

9. _____ 14K   I. light bulb

10. _____ 15-1/2–33   J. timepiece

11. _____ 6 months   K. metric length

12. _____ 4 hp   L. nails

13. _____ AA   M. visual acuity

14. _____ Petite   N. motor

15. _____ 6d   O. tire

16. _____ 50 degrees F   P. gold

17. _____ 100 K RAM   Q. batteries

18. _____ 10 dkm   R. shoes

19. _____ 13 oz   S. lumber

20. _____ 20/20   T. liquid capacity

© 1996 by The Center for Applied Research in Education

4-42   ROMAN NUMERAL FUN

Below is a list of some of the Roman numerals and their more familiar equivalents. Using these clues, see if you can make words by substituting letters for the Roman numerals.

I	=	1		IX	=	9
II	=	2		X	=	10
III	=	3		XI	=	11
IV	=	4		L	=	50
V	=	5		C	=	100
VI	=	6		D	=	500
VII	=	7		M	=	1000
VIII	=	8				

1. 1000/O/500/E/50 _____

2. 500/O/1000/E _____

3. 5/9/EN _____

4. 6/50/E _____

5. 6/1000 _____

6. 1000/1/500/500/50/E _____

7. 1000/O/5/1/E _____

8. 6/500/EO _____

9. 50/4/1/500 _____

10. TA/11 _____

11. 10/-RAY _____

12. 6/OLET _____

13. 500/4/E _____

14. 100/1/6/50 _____

15. E/11/T _____

16. 100/O/500/E _____

17. 500/4/1/500/E _____

18. 1000/1/50/50 _____

4-43   WORLD CURRENCIES

Use the code to find out the currencies of these nations.

1. Japan _____

2. United States _____

3. Italy _____

4. Iraq _____

5. India _____

6. Germany _____

7. China _____

8. Mexico _____

9. France _____

10. South Africa _____

11. Spain _____

12. Sweden _____

13. United Kingdom _____

A ☐ B ◹ C ◔ D ◹ E ◺ F ◺ G ◺ H ☰ I ◫

J ⊞ K ⊠ L ⊠ M ⊠ N ⊠ O ⊠ P ◓ Q ◓ R ◧

S ◧ T ⊞ U ⊞ V ⊞ W ⊞ X ◪ Y Ⅲ Z ☰

© 1996 by The Center for Applied Research in Education

4-44 GEOMETRIC SHAPES

Each geometric shape below is missing some letters. Use the FRONTS and BACKS lists to help you spell them correctly. Cross out each front and back as you use it. You will use them all.

1. ___ ___ U A ___ ___

2. ___ ___ T A G ___ ___

3. ___ ___ I A N G ___ ___

4. ___ ___ L I P ___ ___

5. ___ ___ R C ___ ___

6. ___ ___ C T A N G ___ ___

7. ___ ___ N T A G ___ ___

8. ___ ___ X A G ___ ___

FRONTS			
TR	CI	SQ	HE
RE	OC	PE	EL

BACKS			
LE	LE	LE	SE
ON	ON	ON	RE

189

4-45 WHAT SHAPE ARE YOU IN?

To the Teacher: Run off four sheets of the shapes on tagboard. Cut into cards of equal size. Laminate, if possible. You should have four cards of each shape, a total of 32 cards.

Materials Needed:

- WHAT SHAPE ARE YOU IN? (GAME BOARD)
- WHAT SHAPE ARE YOU IN? (CARDS)
- 1 marker for each player

Number of Players: 2 to 4

How to Play: Stack the cards. Each player draws one card in turn and moves marker to nearest unoccupied shape on the board that is the same as that shown on the card. Player then puts the card on the bottom of the pack.

If a player moves to an incorrect shape and another player notices it, the offending player must return to the beginning star. If a player lands on an occupied shape, the player who was already there must go back to the first unoccupied shape that is the same as the player was on. If the player lands on a plus or negative numbered shape, the player moves forward or backward accordingly.

The object of the game is to get to the end star first.

Rationale: It is hoped that by continually seeing the shapes, their names and spellings, students will become more familiar and remember the difference among common geometric forms.

Modification: Other forms can be pasted over the ones shown to either eliminate or add to the possibilities, depending upon what shapes you want the students to learn or review.

© 1996 by The Center for Applied Research in Education

WHAT SHAPE ARE YOU IN? (GAME BOARD)

BEGIN

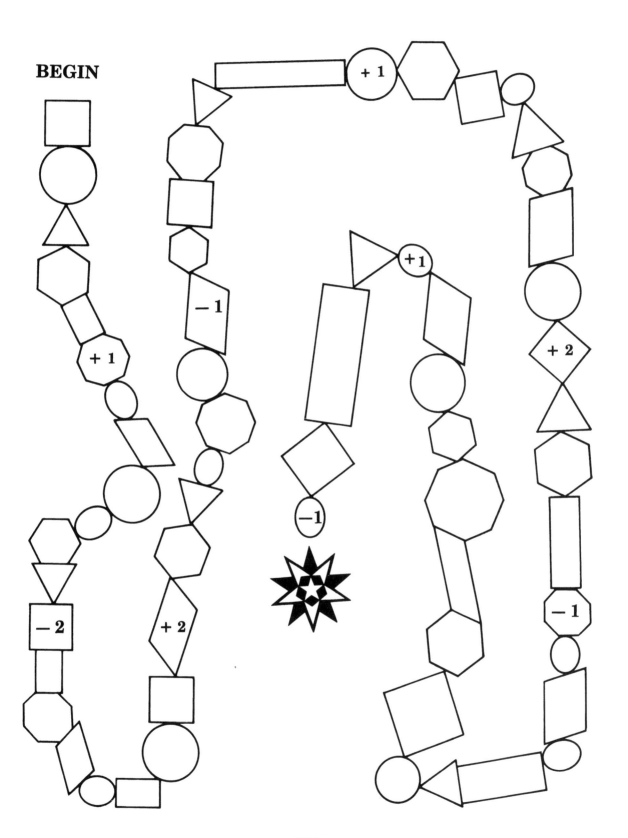

191

WHAT SHAPE ARE YOU IN? (CARDS)

SQUARE	CIRCLE
RECTANGLE	TRIANGLE
OCTAGON	HEXAGON
OVAL	PARALLELOGRAM

4-46   **SOUNDS OF MUSIC**

Across

3. loud
7. highest female voice
9. device to sound beats
10. high, unnatural voice
11. three or more tones together
12. performance by two
14. written symbol for a tone
16. tones sounded together

Down

1. speed
2. four performers
3. stringed-instrument finger guide
4. performing group
5. five lines for notes
6. lower-type female voice
8. interval of eight
9. tune
11. ending
13. type of 3-note chord
15. highest male voice

SOUNDS OF MUSIC

note	soprano	tempo	staff	chord	coda	duet
melody	metronome	quartet	fret	harmony	ensemble
forte	triad	falsetto	tenor	octave	contralto

4-47   SCRAMBLED MUSIC FORMS

Music compositions usually follow a musical <u>form.</u> Unscramble the different types of music using the words in MUSIC FORMS to help you.

1. t h e m a n   _____

2. i r a a   _____

3. l a b l a d   _____

4. a t a n c a t   _____

5. c o r n o t c e   _____

6. g u f u e   _____

7. g a l r i m a d   _____

8. t e n m u i   _____

9. t u r n c o e n   _____

10. t o r r e v u e   _____

11. p r e d u e l   _____

12. q u t t e a r   _____

13. y r h p s o d a   _____

14. r u d o n   _____

15. t a a s o n   _____

MUSIC FORMS

sonata	anthem	prelude	minuet	madrigal
quartet	fugue	nocturne	ballad	round
cantata	aria	overture	concerto	rhapsody

4-48   MUSICAL TEASE

The percussion section of an orchestra contains instruments that are struck with the hands, fingers, or something else to produce a musical sound. Show that you can sort out the percussion instruments from the others shown in the scrambled diagram below. Shade all percussion instruments with pencil or color them one color.

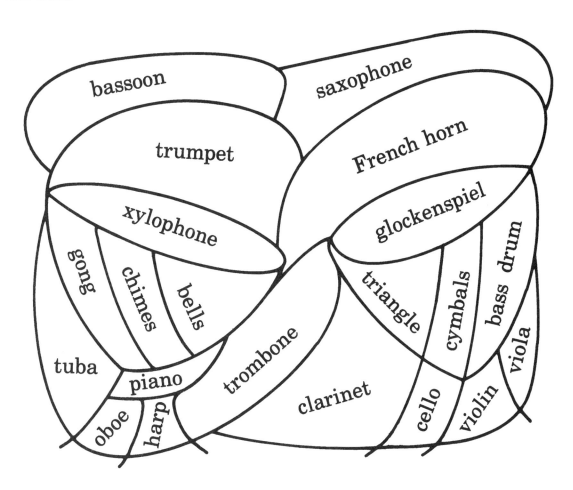

Use the <u>T's</u> clues below to help you write the two names of the major percussion instrument you revealed.

                T   T

___ ___ ___ ___ ___ ___ ___ ___ ___

                T

___ ___ ___ ___ ___ ___ ___

4-49   ORCHESTRA PIT

The musical instruments in the ORCHESTRA PIT are hiding within the sentences below. The instruments may be hidden within one word or several words, but the letters will be in order. Ignore commas; capital letters may be used like small letters. Circle the names of the instruments in the sentences.

Example: Chi Chi Mesito was a great athlete.

(This sentence hides the word <u>chimes,</u> which can be an instrument in the percussion section of an orchestra.)

1. The bass violently resisted my attempt to catch him.

2. Dances like the mambas and rumbas soon became popular.

3. The cell of the prisoner was not too comfortable.

4. Clari netted her first fish on Sunday.

5. His rancor nettled his enemies.

6. Marvin was afraid of American bees and English hornets.

7. One of Char's favorite magazines was <u>Harper's Bazaar.</u>

8. No Boeing 747 flies with just a few passengers.

9. The topic, <u>Colonial History,</u> was named by the teacher.

10. John Phillip Sousa phoned his mother regularly.

11. In the maelstrom bones were strewn about.

12. Tim Panisford was my best friend.

13. Three men in a tub are two too many.

© 1996 by The Center for Applied Research in Education

ORCHESTRA PIT

tuba		sousaphone		clarinet
timpani	cello	oboe	cornet	bassoon
English horn	harp	bass viol	piccolo	trombone

4-50   ANCIENT INSTRUMENTS

Many ancient instruments are no longer played, but many <u>are.</u> From the list below, pick out the old instruments that are still in common use today. To help you, any letters that are connected to each other by lines are the same letter.

bagpipe	harpsichord	organ	sitar
cello	krummhorn	piano	timpani
clavichord	lute	psaltery	viol
dulcimer	lyre	recorder	violin
harp	ophicleide	shawm	zither

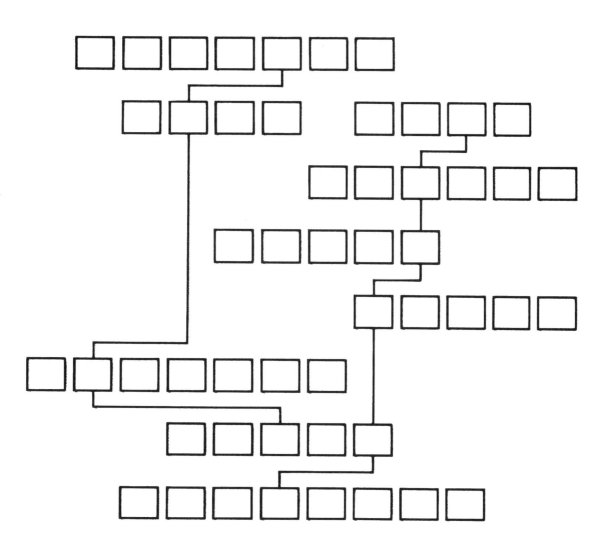

4-51 NATIVE AMERICAN DANCES (SET I)

Native American dances varied depending on the part of the country. Most groups had social powwow dances; other dances revolved around work, games, rain, prayer, harvest, hunting, whaling, burial, war, and weddings. Chanting, rattles, shakers, scrapers, masks, headdresses, and costumes were popular.

Use the code to identify some of the dances these Native American groups enjoyed.

A (1)	F (6)	K (11)	P (16)	U (21)
B (2)	G (7)	L (12)	Q (17)	V (22)
C (3)	H (8)	M (13)	R (18)	W (23)
D (4)	I (9)	N (14)	S (19)	Y (24)
E (5)	J (10)	O (15)	T (20)	Z (25)

Native American Group   **Types of Dances**

1. East Woodlands Iroquois   12/15/14/7-8/15/21/19/5

   _____

2. West Great Basin and Plains   7/8/15/19/20

   _____

3. Hopi and Zuni   3/15/18/14

   _____

4. Plains; Arapaho; Cheyenne;   19/21/14
   Dakota Sioux; Omaha;
   Pawnee; Wichita
                                              _____

5. Plateau Region   19/23/1/14

   _____

6. Alaska Athabascan   16/15/20/12/1/29/3/8

   _____

7. Southwest Yaqui   3/5/5/18

   _____

8. Eskimo   13/9/13/5

   _____

© 1996 by The Center for Applied Research in Education

4-52 NATIVE AMERICAN DANCES (SET II)

Native American dances varied depending on the part of the country. Most groups had social powwow dances; other dances revolved around work, games, rain, prayer, harvest, hunting, whaling, burial, war, and weddings. Chanting, rattles, shakers, scrapers, masks, headdresses, and costumes were popular.

Use the code to identify some of the dances these Native American groups enjoyed.

A (1)	F (6)	K (11)	P (16)	U (21)
B (2)	G (7)	L (12)	Q (17)	V (22)
C (3)	H (8)	M (13)	R (18)	W (23)
D (4)	I (9)	N (14)	S (19)	Y (24)
E (5)	J (10)	O (15)	T (20)	Z (25)

Native American Group   **Types of Dances**

1. Plains   23/1/18

_____

2. East Woodlands   19/20/15/13/16

_____

3. Hopi of Northeast Arizona   19/14/1/11/5

_____

4. Pacific Northwest   19/20/15/18/24

_____

5. Chickasaw; Creek   7/18/5/5/14   3/15/18/14

_____

6. Plains Caddo   20/21/18/11/5/24

_____

7. Northwest Yakima   2/21/20/20/5/18/6/12/24

_____

8. Southwest Pima   2/1/19/11/5/20

_____

4-53   AFRICAN-AMERICAN INFLUENCE
ON MUSIC AND DANCE

Below are several pairs of music and dance types. From each pair, pick out the one that the African-American community had the most influence upon. Then write the words in the puzzle.

1. jazz
   folk

2. bebop
   opera

3. waltz
   blues

4. rap
   pop

5. adagio
   hip hop

6. boogie
   bolero

7. shimmy
   square

4-54   SPANISH AND LATINO INFLUENCE ON MUSIC AND DANCE

Below are several pairs of music and dance types. From each pair, pick out the one that the Spanish or Latino community had the most influence upon. Then write the words in the puzzle.

1. conga
   polka

2. waltz
   rumba

3. volta
   samba

4. minuet
   cha cha

5. salsa
   march

6. calypso
   country

7. twist
   tango

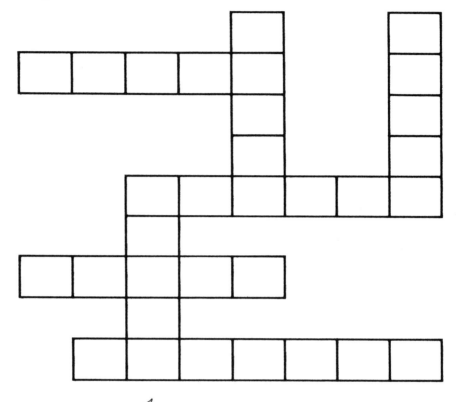

4-55   DECODE THE BALLET

Decode the ballet terms from the BALLET BANK. Find a letter that stands for each number by using the clue word to break the code. Put the correct letters in the blanks.

CLUE WORD:

B	A	L	L	E	R	I	N	A
25	26	15	15	22	9	18	13	26

1. A D A G I O
   26 23 26 20 18 12

2. A R A B E S Q U E
   26 9 26 25 22 8 10 6 22

3. C A B R I O L E
   24 26 25 9 18 12 15 22

4. E L E V A T I O N
   22 15 22 5 26 7 18 12 13

5. L E O T A R D
   15 22 12 7 26 9 23

6. J E T E
   17 22 7 22

7. P L I E
   11 15 18 22

8. P O I N T E
   11 12 18 13 7 22

9. P O S I T I O N S
   11 12 8 18 7 18 12 13 8

10. T U T U
    7 6 7 6

BALLET BANK

tutu	arabesque
jete	leotard
plie	positions
pointe	cabriole
adagio	elevation

4-56 COLOR ME RED

Shade in or color red any boxes with the same number as a <u>shade</u> of the color <u>red.</u> When you finish, the shaded area will look like the last letter in the color.

1	2	3	4
5	6	7	8
9	10	11	12
13	14	15	16
17	18	19	20

1. crimson

2. scarlet

3. carmine

4. garnet

5. aquamarine

6. magenta

7. azure

8. coral

9. navy

10. wine

11. beige

12. vermillion

13. ecru

14. rose

15. taupe

16. cerise

17. burgundy

18. ruby

19. carnation

20. maroon

4-57   PAINTING STYLES

Figure out the painting styles of these famous artists by using three types of clues: shape of letters; number of letters; and repetition of circled letters. Write styles in boxes.

1. K(a)ndinsky

2. Rub(e)ns

3. Reno(i)r

4. d(a) Vinci

5. Mati(s)se

6. (D)uchamp

7. El Gr(e)co

8. Bocc(i)oni

9. Cou(r)bet

10. Pollo(c)k

11. Pica(s)so

12. D(a)vid

13. R(o)uault

14. Dal(i)

15. van G(o)gh

PAINTING STYLES

postimpressionism

impressionism

dadaism   mannerism

realism   action

cubism   surrealism

renaissance

neoclassicism

futurism   baroque

abstract   fauvism

expressionism

4-58   LIGHTS! CAMERA! ACTION!

Use the THEATER TERMS to fill in the words in the story.

The (1)_____ called, "(2)_____"
and the (3)_____ and (4)_____ took
their places on the (5)_____. The
(6)_____ was quiet, the (7)_____ rose,
and the (8)_____ began.

The first (9)_____ made her (10)_____.
Her beautiful, ruffled (11)_____, skillfully applied
(12)_____, and clever (13)_____
fooled everyone.

At one point the (14)_____ made a mistake and the
(15)_____ fell over. The (16)_____
was ruined! But the plucky (17)_____ kept on until the
(18)_____ lights dimmed and the actors came
(19)_____ to take their final
(20)_____ _____.

Although everyone had (21)_____ the best they could,
the (22)_____ had written so much
(23)_____ in the (24)_____ that it
made the (25)_____ very hard to learn. They often missed
their (26)_____ even though there was a
(27)_____ to whisper help.

As they made their (28)_____ from the
(29)_____, everyone was glad it was over. What was
supposed to be a (30)_____ turned out to be a
(31)_____ of errors.

THEATER TERMS

rehearsed	tragedy	stage	scenery	downstage	dialog
cues	stagehand	director	audience	playwright	actors
exit	entrance	prompter	curtain call	house	costume
Action	actresses	character	disguise	cast	script
makeup	comedy	play	theater	lines	curtain
					set

4-59   ADDITION AND SUBTRACTION

The answers in this word puzzle all are related to one thing. Add and subtract letters to get the answers. Then write one word that all these words are related to at the bottom of the page.

Hint: You must add letters only to the ending of the word and subtract letters only from left to right!

1. daydream − da + a − ye = _____

2. accost + u − c + me − a = _____

3. tractor − t + e − r − e = _____

4. prehearing − ing + s − p + al = _____

5. welcome − w + d − l + y − e = _____

6. scale − a + ne − l + ry = _____

7. react + re − re + ss = _____

8. system − sy + ag − em + e = _____

9. surprise − ise + ope − sur + rty = _____

10. trailer − il + ge − er + dy = _____

WORDS ARE RELATED TO   _____

Name _____

4-60   THE PLAY'S THE THING

Finish the puzzle by using words related to the theater. Fill in each square with <u>one</u> of the three letters in the code guide. Use the definitions in the BALCONY to help you.

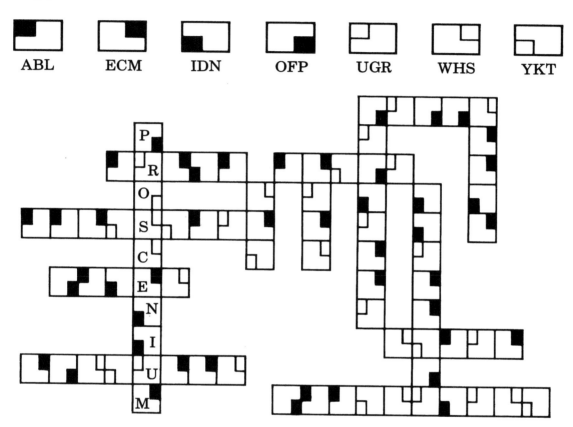

ABL   ECM   IDN   OFP   UGR   WHS   YKT

© 1996 by The Center for Applied Research in Education

Balcony:

Clothes and wigs the people wear
Person who acts
Author of play
Person who raises money, selects play, and pays bills
Arch framing stage
Stage for theater-in-the-round
Space behind the stage (off stage)
Properties (shortened form)
Space above the stage used for lights and storing flats
A smaller part of an act
Offstage workers as a group
Platform on which people perform
Arrangement of scenery and properties on stage
Person who casts characters and oversees rehearsals

207

Section Five

LIBRARY AND REFERENCE

5-1   CARD CATALOG CROSS OUT

Put an <u>X</u> on the square of each drawer in which you would find card catalog cards for the following books. Write whether the card is an author, title, or subject card on the line. When you finish, you should have the shape of the first letter of where the card catalog is found. Spell that place here.

_____ _____ _____ _____ _____ _____ _____

A-AM	D	I	N	SN-SZ
AN-AZ	E	J	O	T
B-BM	F-FM	K	P	U
BN-BZ	FN-FZ	L	Q	V
C-CM	G	M-MM	R	W-X
CN-CZ	H	MM-MZ	S-SM	Y-Z

1. A book about elephants   _____

2. A book by Farley Mowat   _____

3. <u>The Great Waldo Search</u>   _____

4. A book by Virginia Hamilton   _____

5. A book about Denmark   _____

6. <u>Frankenstein</u>   _____

7. A book about zoos   _____

8. <u>Sarah, Plain and Tall</u>   _____

9. A book by Walter Farley   _____

5-2   LIBRARY SKILLS REVIEW

Follow the directions and find a secret message on the lines.

___   ___   ___   ___   ___   ___   ___   ___   ___   ___   ___   ___   ___   ___   ___
1   2   3   4   5   6   7   8   9   10   11   12   13   14   15

1. If a book of maps is an atlas, put a T on 6. If not, put an M on 6.

2. If subject listings for a book are called an index, put an R on 12 and 14. If not, put an S on 12 and 14.

3. If a, an, and the are alphabetized in computer and traditional card catalogs, put an F on 13. If not, put an A on 13.

4. If the call number is located on the upper right corner of the author card, put an N on 1 and 3. If not, do nothing.

5. If topics in encyclopedias are arranged alphabetically, put a J on 3. If not, put a J on 15.

6. If a book of facts is an atlas, put a V on 7. If not, put an H on 7.

7. If numbers and letters on the spine are call numbers, put a Y on 5 and 15. If not, put a D on 2.

8. If the types of cards in a card catalog are author, title, and alphabet, put a C on 7. If not, put a B on 11.

9. If magazines and newspapers are biographies, put a B on 6. If not, put an L on 9.

10. If books about another person's life are biographies, put an I on 10. If not, put an L on 5 and 15.

11. If made-up stories are fiction, put an E on 1 and 8. If not, put an A on 1.

12. If true stories are fiction, put a Z on 13. If not, do nothing.

13. If fantasy is nonfiction, put an I on 3. If not, put an O on 4.

14. If a book of facts is an almanac, put an N on 2. If not, put a P on 14.

© 1996 by The Center for Applied Research in Education

Name _____

5-3 MORSE CODE LIBRARY TERMS

Samuel F. B. Morse invented a system of dots and dashes used to represent letters and other items. The code has been modified and used internationally to send messages by telegraph and other means. Below are the dot-dash symbols for each letter of the Morse code alphabet. Use the code to figure out common library terms.

a	· —	j	· — — —	s	· · ·		
b	— · · ·	k	— · —	t	—		
c	— · — ·	l	· — · ·	u	· · —		
d	— · ·	m	— —	v	· · · —		
e	·	n	— ·	w	· — —		
f	· · — ·	o	— — —	x	— · · —		
g	— — ·	p	· — — ·	y	— · — —		
h	· · · ·	q	— — · —	z	— — · ·		
i	· ·	r	· — ·				

1. _____

2. _____

3. _____

4. _____

5. _____

6. _____

213

5-4   DEWEY DECIMAL SUBCATEGORIES

Place the <u>numbers</u> of the topics under the Dewey Decimal System classifications where they would be located in the library. You may use the dictionary, library, card catalog, or computer catalog to help you, if needed.

Hint: Some are tricky. If you do it correctly, though, each category will add up to 40!

1. Architecture
2. Mathematics
3. Engineering
4. Building Construction
5. Music

6. Home Economics
7. Chemistry
8. Astronomy
9. Sculpture
10. Physics

11. Photography
12. Medical Science
13. Paleontology
14. Painting
15. Manufactures

500-599 **PURE SCIENCE**	**600-699** **TECHNOLOGY**	**700-799** **THE ARTS**
_____	_____	_____
_____	_____	_____
_____	_____	_____
_____	_____	_____
_____	_____	_____
Total _____	Total _____	Total _____

© 1996 by The Center for Applied Research in Education

5-5   BIOGRAPHIES

Biographies are on library shelves alphabetically by the last name of the person the book is about (NOT the author's last name!). Put these biographies in the order they would appear on the shelves. Use the <u>numbers</u> for your answers.

Hint: If biographies are in correct order, every pair will add up to 11.

1. Lou Gehrig: An American Hero by Paul Gallico

2. The Life of Charlotte Brontë by Elizabeth Gaskell

3. Abraham Lincoln: The Prairie Years by Carl Sandburg

4. Bruce Springsteen by Peter Gambacuni

5. Judy Blume's Story by Betsy Lee

6. Alan Alda: An Unauthorized Biography by Jason Bonderoff

7. Laura Ingalls Wilder: Growing Up in the Little House by Patricia Riley Giff

8. Let the Trumpet Sound: The Life of Martin Luther King by Stephen B. Oates

9. The Voyages of Columbus by Armstrong Perry

10. The Life of Sir Arthur Conan Doyle by John Dickson Carr

In order on the library shelves:

___ ___   ___ ___   ___ ___   ___ ___   ___ ___

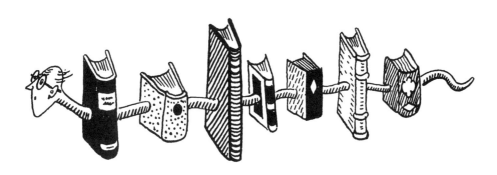

5-6 ENCYCLOPEDIA TOPICS

See if you can unscramble the words below. When rearranged correctly they will list the ten subjects students most frequently look up in the library (according to <u>World Book Encyclopedia</u>).

Hints: All are living things except one.
Six are common pets.
One is a sport.
One is a very important person.

1. _____ shif

2. _____ act

3. _____ kenas

4. _____ manlia

5. _____ bellasab

6. _____ seroh

7. _____ rosindua

8. _____ god

9. _____ stirepend

10. _____ dirb

Extra Credit:

Which would come first in the alphabet? _____

Which would come last in the alphabet? _____

5-7   SEE ALSO

When looking up subjects in an encyclopedia or card catalog, it is sometimes necessary to try a different subject heading than the one that first comes to mind. Match the letter of various subject headings that might be a "See" or "See also" reference. If you do your matching correctly, the answer letters will form a word downward.

_____ 1. TV sets

E. ANATOMY

_____ 2. jets

L. HUMOR

_____ 3. trains

X. AIRPLANES; AERONAUTICS

_____ 4. farms

E. TELEVISION; COMMUNICATION

_____ 5. cartoons

T. PHYSICIANS

_____ 6. Corvettes

E. AGRICULTURE

_____ 7. face

N. ADOLESCENCE

_____ 8. teenagers

L. AUTOMOBILES; TRANSPORTATION

_____ 9. doctors

C. RAILROADS; TRANSPORTATION

5-8 SAY WHAT? BETTER CHECK THE DICTIONARY!

Literary humor often relies on a play on words. These medical terms have interesting plays on words. Use the dictionary to look up definitions of the words and write brief meanings on the lines.

WORDS	PLAYS ON WORDS	DEFINITIONS
1. artery	study of painting	_____
2. barium	to do after death	_____
3. bowels	a, e, i, o,u	_____
4. CAT scan	search for kitty	_____
5. cauterize	made eye contact	_____
6. dilate	to live long	_____
7. enema	not a friend	_____
8. fester	quicker	_____
9. morbid	higher offer	_____
10. nitrates	less than day rates	_____
11. node	was aware of	_____
12. outpatient	person who fainted	_____
13. Pap smear	fatherhood test	_____
14. pelvis	cousin to Elvis	_____
15. postoperative	letter carrier	_____
16. rectum	nearly ruined 'em	_____
17. seizure	Roman emperor	_____
18. terminally ill	sick at airport	_____
19. tumor	addition of two	_____
20. urine	when not out	_____
21. varicose	nearby	_____
22. vein	conceited	_____

5-9 WORDS THAT CAME FROM PEOPLE

These people all had words named after them. Put the WORDS in the puzzle.

1. Louis Braille

2. Charles Boycott

3. Mae West

4. Amelia Bloomer

5. Captain Shaddock

6. Samuel E. Maverick

7. John Montagu, 4th Earl of Sandwich

8. Diedrich Knickerbocker (Washington Irving)

9. Adolphe Sax

10. Louis Pasteur

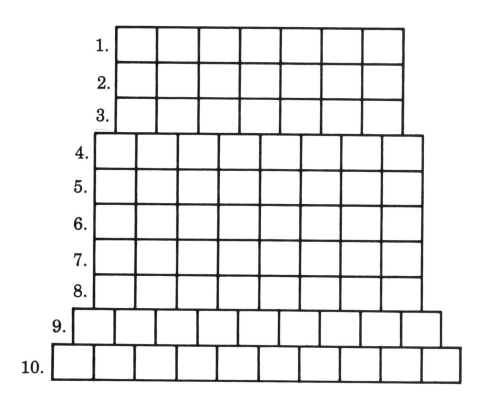

© 1996 by The Center for Applied Research in Education

5-10 WORDS THAT CAME FROM VARIOUS COUNTRIES

With your partner, look up the origin of the word your teacher assigns you. As you find it, put the word and the COUNTRY where it originated on the chalkboard. When you finish, find <u>other</u> words (not on the list) that have a country of origin that is NOT on the chalkboard yet. Add your new word to the chalkboard list to see how many different countries of origin you can find.

Hint: If several origins are listed in the dictionary, be sure to keep reading until the final listing. If you find unfamiliar symbols or abbreviations, use the dictionary key usually found in the front of the book to help you. Some common abbreviations of origins and the countries they represent:

AmInd	American Indian (America)
Chin	Chinese (China)
F	French (France)
G	German (Germany)
Gk	Greek (Greece)
Ir	Irish (Ireland)
It	Italian (Italy)
L	Latin (Ancient Rome)
LL	Late Latin (Roman Empire)
ME	Middle English (England)
OE	Old English (England)
Sp	Spanish (Spain)

1. zigzag _____

2. autograph _____

3. captain _____

4. deceit _____

5. fascism _____

6. gaucho _____

7. chow (food) _____

8. mademoiselle _____

9. babushka _____

10. kimono _____

11. terrapin _____

12. taffeta _____

13. kosher _____

14. kayak _____

15. marimba _____

5-11 NAMES AND THEIR ORIGINS

Names of people often have meanings relating to their origins. Most names are based on places, occupations, months, planets, gods and goddesses, titles, colors, jewels, flowers, Biblical characters, historical figures, or personality characteristics.

From the list below, pick out a name for yourself <u>based on its original meaning only.</u> Try to pick a name whose meaning describes YOU best. The rest of the class will try to decide what name you picked. Whoever guesses correctly gets to have others guess his or her picked name (or if the student has already had a turn, can choose the next player). The student or teacher can call on students who raise hands to guess.

Note: First form listed is usually a girl; second name is usually a boy; origin is in parentheses; meaning is last. If only one name is given, the same form is common for both boys and girls.

Akiko/Akio (Japanese)—bright
Alana/Alan (Irish-Gaelic)—handsome
Alex (French/Greek)—defender
Ali (Arabic)—the greatest
Blair (Scottish/Gaelic)—battlefield
Blake (Old English)—fair-haired
Cameron (Gaelic)—bent nose
Carey (Welsh/Celtic)—loving
Casey (Irish)—alert
Cassidy (Irish/Welsh)—curly-headed
Chris (Latin)—Christian
Cody (Irish/Gaelic)—helpful
Dakota (American Indian)—friend
Daryl (English/French)—open
Devon (English)—perfect
Dorian (Greek)—gift
Georganne/George (Latin)—farmer

Hilary (Greek)—cheerful
Kali (Sanskrit)—energy
Karla/Carl (Old German)—strong
Kelly (Gaelic/Irish)—lively
Kerry (Irish/Gaelic)—dark-haired
Kim (English)—precious gold
Leslie (Scottish)—royalty
Loren (Spanish/Italian)—notable
Mackenzie (Gaelic/Scottish)—favored
Maxine/Max (English)—the greatest
Paula/Paul (Latin)—small
Philipa/Philip (Greek)—horse-lover
Pilar (Spanish)—pillar
Quinn (Gaelic/Irish)—counselor
Robin (English)—bright; famous
Shannon (Gaelic/Irish)—wise
Terry (Germanic)—powerful

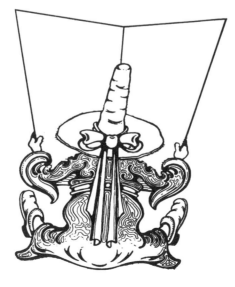

5-12 LOCATION RELAY

To the Teacher: Divide class into four teams of six or less people. (If you have more people on a team, repeat one or more of the letters in the card pack.)

Divide alphabet cards into four card packs (six cards to a pack). Place alphabet cards at front of room or equi-distant from each team.

Number of Players: Entire class

Materials Needed: • Library
• ALPHABET CARDS
• Construction paper or other markers to put in shelves where book is removed

How to Play: First student for each team takes card from team's card pack to see what letter to use to find a fiction book (with the last name of the author starting with that letter). Paper markers must be placed where the book is taken out.

These four students return to their seats with their books. The first to return and be seated scores one point. Then the second team members repeat the procedure, again with the fastest locator to return to his or her seat gaining a point for his or her team. Continue until all team members have found a correct fiction book.

Students then pass the books and cards one back (or to the right if around a table). First team member passes both book and card to second team member and so on with last team member passing his or her book and card to first team member. Students proceed to return books (all students at once) with the first FULL team returning to their seats without books, but with their cards and paper markers, scoring five points. The team with the most total points from both finding and returning books wins the game.

Rationale: This is a great game to familiarize students with where fiction is located in the library. Without even realizing it, they are reinforcing the idea that fiction is located on the shelves alphabetically by the last name of the author, a skill they will need in every library they frequent.

Additionally, not all the pressure is put on an individual student, but rather a team effort is emphasized. The activity provides actual hands-on experience and seems to hold the attention of most groups. Students gain confidence in locating fiction as they play the game repeatedly throughout the school year.

Modification: If you want to make this an easier game for students less familiar with the library, have them eliminate the step of passing their books and markers to another student. Let them return their own book to where they found it and bring their shelf marker back. Again, the first team to return to their seats with the markers is the winning team.

ALPHABET CARDS

A	B
C	D
E	F
G	H

I	J
K	L
M	N
O	P

Q	R
S	T
U	V
W	X

ALPHABET CARDS
(Cont'd)

Y	**Z**
A	**B**
C	**D**
E	**F**

5-13 DEWEY DECIMAL REVIEW

To the Teacher: Run off one copy of each SAMPLE DEWEY CARDS sheet. Cut into cards. Laminate, if possible. This game will involve 16 or more students directly. If you want to play another "round," call on 8 students who have not been up in front to begin the next game. It is assumed students have been taught the rudiments of decimal division prior to this game.

Number of Players: Entire class

Materials Needed: • SAMPLE DEWEY CARDS

How to Play: Eight students line up. Give each one a SAMPLE DEWEY CARD to put in front of him or her so the class can see. The cards should be out of order.

Call on a student from the "audience." The student changes places with the standing student who holds the card that should come first and puts self (with card) in correct numerical order. The order should read left to right from the audience point of view.

The student who sits down calls on another student to exchange with the student holding the next correct numerical card. This continues until students standing are holding all cards in correct numerical order. If a student makes an error, a subsequent student can correct it using the same procedure.

Rationale: This review is designed to give students an actual kinesthetic experience reviewing decimals and their order. This is a tough but necessary concept for kids, and the more concrete you can make it, instead of an abstraction, the more easily they will learn it.

Modification: You can make other cards, harder or easier depending upon the group, to substitute or add to these cards.

Sample Dewey Cards

841.25

841.28

841

841.26

841.288

842

841.283

841.3

5-14   DEWEY RELAY

To the Teacher: Divide class into four teams of six or less people. (If you have more people on a team, repeat one or more of the letters in the card pack.)

Run off both pages of SELECTED DEWEY CARDS. Divide cards into four card packs (six cards to a pack). Place SELECTED DEWEY CARDS at front of room or equi-distant from each team.

Players: Entire class

Materials Needed:
- Library
- SELECTED DEWEY CARDS—2 pages
- Construction paper or other markers to put in shelves where book is removed

How to Play: First student for each team takes card from team's card pack to see what call number to use to find a nonfiction book. Paper markers must be placed where the book is taken out.

These four students return to their seats with their books. The first to return and be seated scores one point for the team. Then the second team members repeat the procedure, again with the fastest locator to be seated gaining a point for his or her team. Continue until all team members find a correct nonfiction book.

Pass the books and cards one back (or to the right if around a table). First team member passes both book and card to second team member and so on with last team member passing his or her book and card to first team member. Then proceed to return books (all students at once). The first FULL team returning to their seats without books, but with their cards and paper markers, scores five points for their team. The team with the most total points from locating and returning books wins the game.

Rationale: This is a great game to familiarize students with where nonfiction is located in the library. Without even realizing it, they are reinforcing the idea that nonfiction is located on the shelves by call numbers, using decimals, which represent subject categories.

Additionally, not all the pressure is put on an individual student, but rather a team effort is emphasized. The activity provides actual hands-on experience and seems to hold the attention of most age groups. Students gain confidence in locating nonfiction as they play the game repeatedly throughout the school year.

Modification: If you want to make this an easier game for students less familiar with the library, have them eliminate the step of passing their books and markers to another student. Let them return their own book to where they found it and bring their shelf marker back. Again, the first team to return to their seats with their markers is the winning team.

SELECTED DEWEY CARDS

796 **OUTDOOR SPORTS**	**621.3** **COMPUTERS**
398.2 **FAIRY TALES**	**636.8** **CATS**
523 **STARS**	**598.2** **BIRDS**
629.1 **PLANES**	**745.5** **CRAFTS**
636.1 **HORSES**	**552** **ROCKS**
970.3 **AMERICAN INDIANS**	**808.8** **JOKES**
636.7 **DOGS**	**629.2** **CARS/CYCLES**

SELECTED DEWEY CARDS
(Cont'd)

594 SHELLS	796.2 SKATING
628 POLLUTION	597.3 SHARKS
799.1 FISHING	599.8 MONKEYS
786 MUSICAL INSTRUMENTS	743 DRAWING
553.8 GEMS	629.4 OUTER SPACE
972 MEXICO	394.2 HOLIDAYS
385.09 TRAINS	567.91 DINOSAURS

5-15   ATLAS OR ALMANAC?

To the Teacher: Explain that an atlas is a book of maps and an almanac is a book of facts on many varied subjects. (You might even put the definitions on the board so students can refer to them during the game the first few times they play.)

Run off ATLAS OR ALMANAC? (QUESTIONS) sheets. (The best source for the first page of questions is the almanac; the second page, the atlas. These are listed in the answer key, so you don't have to keep track.) Cut into strips. Fold over, if desired. Mix up the two batches, so each includes atlas and almanac topics. Put an equal number of mixed-up slips into each of the two containers, though not necessarily an equal amount of each type.

Number of Players: Entire class, divided into two teams

Materials Needed: • ATLAS OR ALMANAC? (QUESTIONS)
                                        • 2 containers

How to Play: First members of both teams come to front. Team I member draws slip, reads it to the class, and says either "atlas" or "almanac," depending on which would be the better source to find the information.

If Team II member agrees the answer is correct, Team I member gets one point for the team. If Team II member thinks the answer is not correct, he or she challenges Team I member. If challenged, but correct, Team I member gets the point, and the challenger sits down with no chance to draw a slip or gain a point. If the challenger is right, however, the challenger gets the point. (A point is ALWAYS scored for one of the teams every time a new slip is drawn.)

Both team members sit down, and the next members from each team come forward. The first to draw should alternate between teams. That is, if Team I member drew the first slip, Team II member should draw the first slip the next round; Team I the following round, and so on.

Summary of turn:

1. Draw slip. Read to class.

2. Answer "atlas" or "almanac."

3. Wait for challenge or agreement from opponent.

4. If you get the point, mark it on the chalkboard for your team.

5. Sit down.

Rationale: This game underscores the multitude of information available in both resources and gets students used to saying the terms as well as distinguishing between the two. The aim is NOT to look up the answers to the questions, but rather to make judgments as to the quicker, easier source if one wanted to find the information.

ATLAS OR ALMANAC? (QUESTIONS)

Who won the World Series in 1990?

How many motorcycles are in the United States?

What is the average price that farmers receive for beef?

Who is the mayor of San Francisco?

Who are the senators from your state?

When did your state enter the union?

Who was Miss America in 1926?

What actor won the Oscar for best picture in 1995?

How does the population of your state compare with the other states?

Who was MVP in the Super Bowl in 1994?

What is the capacity of the Metrodome in Minneapolis?

How did your state vote in the last major presidential election?

What amendment to the Constitution lowers the voting age to 18?

Who signed the Declaration of Independence?

Who was the wife of former President Truman?

Who won the first Kentucky Derby in 1875?

Who was NBA Rookie of the Year in 1979?

What is the biggest freshwater fish ever caught?

Who was the heavyweight champion of the world from 1974-1977?

Who won the Major League Baseball Pennant in 1901?

ATLAS OR ALMANAC? (QUESTIONS)
(Cont'd)

How far is it from Chicago to Des Moines?

On what continent is Tanzania?

What states border your state?

Is there a road from Detroit to Mackinac Island, Michigan?

Is Corpus Christi on the Gulf of Mexico?

What is your state shaped like?

Does India border China?

How many provinces are there in Canada?

Which states have a common border with Mexico?

Where is the largest country in South America located?

Is Japan an island or a series of islands?

What are the latitude and longitude of Mongolia?

What countries have a coastline on the Mediterranean Sea?

Where is Iraq?

Is Ireland part of England?

How many continents are there?

Which states have Pacific Ocean coastlines?

Which state is almost surrounded by large, freshwater lakes?

How far is it from Florida to North Dakota?

Where is the major river in Nebraska located?

Section Six

HOLIDAYS AND SEASONS

Name ________________________________

6-1 HOLIDAY CODES

Read the HOLIDAY CODE GRID to find the information about holidays. Find the code numbers and letters on the outside of the grid. Look to see where the code numbers and letters intersect.

1. ____ ____ ____ ____ ____ ____ ____ ____ ____ is December 25.
   2C 3A 5C 5E 1A 5B 3D 1C 1A

2. February 22 is the birthday of ____ ____ ____ ____ ____ ____
   2E 5A 2A 5C 2E 5A

   ____ ____ ____ ____ ____ ____ ____ ____ ____ ____.
   1E 1C 1A 3A 5E 2B 2E 5B 2A 2B

3. New Year's Day is in ____ ____ ____ ____ ____ ____ ____.
   5D 1C 2B 1D 1C 5C 4A

4. March 17 is ____ ____. ____ ____ ____ ____ ____ ____ ____' ____ Day.
   1A 5B 1B 1C 5B 5C 5E 2C 2D 1A

5. February 2 is ____ ____ ____ ____ ____ ____ ____ ____ ____ Day.
   2E 5C 2A 1D 2B 3E 3A 2A 2E

6. Flag Day and Father's Day are in ____ ____ ____ ____.
   5D 1D 2B 5A

7. Veteran's Day is in ____ ____ ____ ____ ____ ____ ____ ____.
   2B 2A 3B 5A 3D 4E 5A 5C

8. The first day of ____ ____ ____ ____ ____ ____ ____ ____ is usually in December.
   3A 1C 2B 1D 2D 2D 1C 3A

9. January 16 is the birthday of ____ ____ ____ ____ ____ ____
   3D 1C 5C 5B 5E 2B

   ____ ____ ____ ____ ____ ____ ____ ____ ____ ____.
   3C 1D 5B 3A 5A 5C 2D 5E 2B 2E

10. Thanksgiving is the ____ ____ ____ ____ ____ ____ Thursday in November.
    4B 2A 1D 5C 5B 3A

5	E	T	R	J	I
4	Y	F	Q	X	B
3	H	V	L	M	D
2	O	N	C	K	G
1	S	P	A	U	W
	A	B	C	D	E

6-2   OCTOBER DAZE

The following things are associated with October. Write them on the calendar where they belong and answer the questions.

1. Daylight Savings Time Ends (4th Sunday)

   Do clocks go forward or back? _____*

2. Halloween (31st)

   Draw a pumpkin here:

3. Columbus Day (observed 2nd Monday)

   What was Columbus's first name? _____

4. Yom Kippur (3rd at sundown—in 1995)

   Who celebrate this holiday? _____

O C T O B E R						
S	**M**	**T**	**W**	**T**	**F**	**S**
1	2	3	4	5	6	7
8	9	10	11	12	13	14
15	16	17	18	19	20	21
22	23	24	25	26	27	28
29	30	31				

* "Spring forward; fall back."

© 1996 by The Center for Applied Research in Education

6-3   HALLOWEEN PUMPKIN

A fact is true and can be proved to be true. An opinion is what someone believes to be true, but cannot be proved.

See how well you know your Halloween pumpkin facts and opinions. Circle **F** if the sentence is a fact. Circle **O** if it is an opinion. Then connect the dots of the numbers of each FACT only. Draw a face on your result.

F   **O**   1. Pumpkins are round.

F   **O**   2. Pumpkins are orange.

F   **O**   3. Pumpkins taste good.

F   **O**   4. People can carve faces on pumpkins.

F   **O**   5. Pumpkin faces are scary.

F   **O**   6. Pumpkin can be made into pie.

F   **O**   7. Pumpkin pie is too spicy.

F   **O**   8. Some pumpkins are larger than others.

F   **O**   9. Some pumpkins are a darker color than others.

F   **O**   10. Some people hollow out pumpkins.

F   **O**   11. Some people put candles in pumpkins.

F   **O**   12. Lighted pumpkins scare ghosts.

Write a pumpkin FACT here: _____

_____

Write a pumpkin OPINION here: _____

_____

          3.   1.   11.   5.

          2.   .   .   10.

          4.   .   .   9.

          7.   6.   8.   12.

6-4   SPECIAL NOVEMBER DAYS

November celebrates several special days as shown in the chart below. Fill in the rest of the chart with words that relate to these holidays.

SPECIAL NOVEMBER DAYS		
THANKSGIVING	VETERANS DAY	ELECTION DAY
4TH THURSDAY	NOVEMBER 11	1ST TUESDAY
1.	1.	1.
2.	2.	2.
3.	3.	3.
4.	4.	4.
5.	5.	5.

Name _____

6-5 DECEMBER DAYS OUTLINE

Many important days are remembered in December. See if you can organize the SCRAMBLED TOPICS into a sensible outline, using the holidays or occasions as main headings (I, II, etc.) and the dates and other details as subordinate points (A, B, etc.).

I. _____

    A. _____

    B. _____

    C. _____

    D. _____

    E. _____

    F. _____

II. _____

    A. _____

    B. _____

    C. _____

    D. _____

    E. _____

III. _____

    A. _____

    B. _____

    C. _____

IV. _____

    A. _____

    B. _____

    C. _____

V. _____

    A. _____

    B. _____

    C. _____

    D. _____

SCRAMBLED TOPICS

December 31	Japanese bombing of Hawaii
Hanukkah	Evergreen trees
December 21	Jewish festival
December (usually)	Menorah
Presents	Colder weather
Pearl Harbor Day	First day of Winter
Year of 1946	December 7
Winter solstice (U.S.)	Official end of WWII
Christian celebration	December 25
Rededication of Temple	Year of 1941
Birth of Christ	Shortest day (U.S.)
8-day celebration	Defeat of the Axis
Santa Claus	Christmas Day

6-6   WINTERTIME FUN

You don't have to be an artist to draw a wintertime picture. Just draw each code square in the corresponding square on the grid.

1C	1D	1E	2C	2D	2E	3B	3C	3D	3E

3F	4A	4B	4C	4D	4E	4F	5A	5B	5C

5D	5E	5F	5G	6A	6B	6D	6F	6G	6H

7A	7F	7G	7H	8A	8G	9A	9G	10A	10G

11A	11B	11E	11F	11G	12B	12C	12D	12E	12F

	A	B	C	D	E	F	G	H
1								
2								
3								
4								
5								
6								
7								
8								
9								
10								
11								
12								

6-7   BROKEN HEARTS OF ART

Hearts are a symbol of Valentine's Day. See if you can put these broken hearts together to form words related to art.

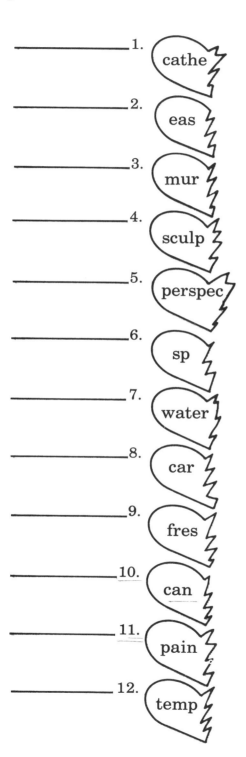

_____ 1. cathe

_____ 2. eas

_____ 3. mur

_____ 4. sculp

_____ 5. perspec

_____ 6. sp

_____ 7. water

_____ 8. car

_____ 9. fres

_____ 10. can

_____ 11. pain

_____ 12. temp

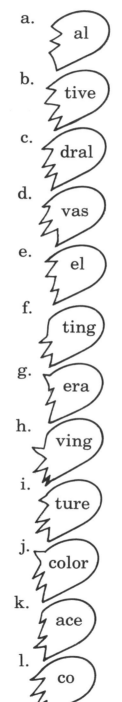

a. al

b. tive

c. dral

d. vas

e. el

f. ting

g. era

h. ving

i. ture

j. color

k. ace

l. co

6-8   ST. PATRICK'S DAY WORDS

Put the correct answers on the lines, and find this holiday symbol.

_____   1. What country is associated with this day?

     r. England
     s. Ireland
     t. Scotland

_____   2. What color is associated with this day?

     f. blue
     g. red
     h. green

_____   3. Which gem is associated with this day?

     a. emerald
     b. ruby
     c. diamond

_____   4. Which plant is associated with this day?

     l. four-leaf clover
     m. shamrock
     n. ivy

_____   5. Where does a famous parade for this day take place?

     r. Boston
     s. London
     t. Paris

_____   6. Saint Patrick's Day is on which date?

     m. March 27
     n. May 7
     o. March 17

_____   7. How many segments are in the symbol for this day?

     b. two
     c. three
     d. four

_____   8. Who was Saint Patrick?

     k. missionary
     l. historian
     m. patrician

© 1996 by The Center for Applied Research in Education

6-9   EASTER "EGGS"

You can answer each of these questions with a word that starts with "eggs" ("ex," that is!). Use the EASTER EGG BASKET to help you. You will not use all the words. Spell YOUR words with <u>ex.</u>

1. What eggs are very precise?   _____

2. What eggs do you have to study for?   _____

3. What eggs give you a "for instance"?   _____

4. What eggs give you a close look?   _____

5. What eggs dig?   _____

6. What eggs are more than you need?   _____

7. What eggs are outstanding?   _____

8. What eggs do you trade?   _____

9. What eggs pep you up?   _____

10. What eggs take you off the hook?   _____

11. What eggs kill?   _____

12. What eggs make you physically fit?   _____

13. What eggs come out of your car?   _____

14. What eggs banish kings?   _____

15. What eggs run out?   _____

EASTER EGG BASKET

	eggsample	eggsterior	eggspress	
eggscellent	eggstinct	eggscuse	eggsecute	eggscavate
eggsercize	eggspand	eggsamine	eggspose	eggschange
eggshaust	eggsit	eggsplode	eggshale	eggscite
eggsact	eggsile	eggspire	eggstra	eggsam

Appendix One

GENERIC AIDS

GAME CARDS

The following four pages contain cards for use in large and small groups. The sheets can be used in a variety of ways, from flash cards, to game cards, to response cards to teacher questions or examples. ALPHABET CARDS and others are located elsewhere near explanations of specific games. The list below details the cards contained in this section.

1. **Types of Sentences and End Punctuation**

   a. Declarative (.)
   b. Interrogative (?)
   c. Exclamatory (!)
   d. Imperative (.)

2. **Other Punctuation**

   a. Comma
   b. Quotation marks
   c. Semi-colon
   d. Colon

3. **Eight Parts of Speech**

   a. Noun
   b. Pronoun
   c. Verb
   d. Adjective
   e. Adverb
   f. Preposition
   g. Conjunction
   h. Interjection

4. **Other**

   a. Helping Verb/Linking Verb/Action Verb
   b. Positive/Comparative/Superlative
   c. Synonym/Antonym
   d. Small Alphabet Letters

To prepare for use:

1. Copy the pages on tagboard and laminate, if feasible; or make the pages with plastic overhead transparencies.

2. Cut cards apart with paper cutter, being sure all cards are of uniform size.

251

GAME CARDS

DECLARATIVE ■	**INTERROGATIVE** **?**
EXCLAMATORY **!**	**IMPERATIVE** ■
COMMA **,**	**QUOTATION MARKS** **" "**
SEMICOLON ■ **,**	**COLON** ■ ■

GAME CARDS
(Continued)

Noun	**Verb**
Adverb	**Conjunction**
Pronoun	**Adjective**
Preposition	**Interjection**

GAME CARDS
(Continued)

Helping Verb	**Action Verb**
Linking Verb	**Positive**
Comparative	**Superlative**
Synonym	**Antonym**

SMALL ALPHABET LETTERS
(number of each according to how common)

A	A	A	A	A	A	A	A	A
E	E	E	E	E	E	E	E	E
E	E	E	I	I	I	I	I	I
I	I	I	O	O	O	O	O	O
O	O	U	U	U	U	U	U	U
B	B	C	C	D	D	D	D	D
F	F	G	G	G	H	H	J	K
L	L	L	L	M	M	M	N	N
N	N	N	N	P	P	Q	R	R
R	R	R	R	R	S	S	S	S
T	T	T	T	T	T	V	V	V
W	W	W	X	Y	Y	Y	Y	Z
A	B	C	D	E	F	G	H	I
J	K	L	M	N	O	P	Q	R
S	T	U	V	W	X	Y	Z	

SPINNER PATTERN

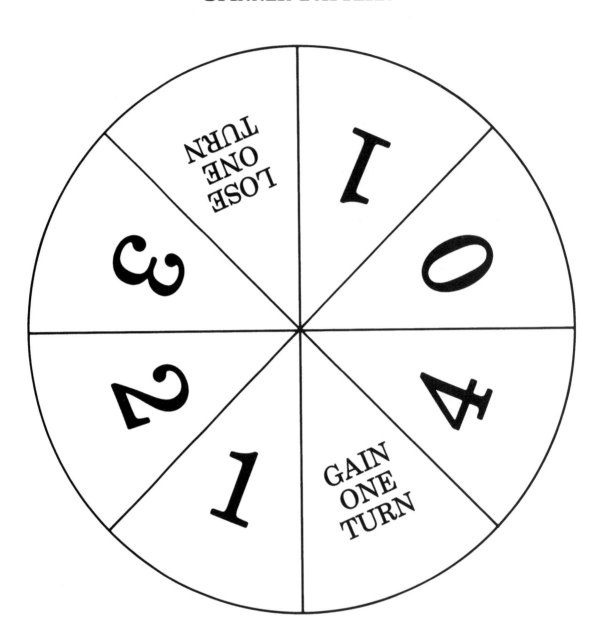

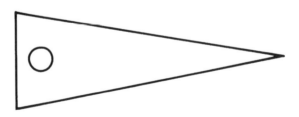

GENERIC SPINNER

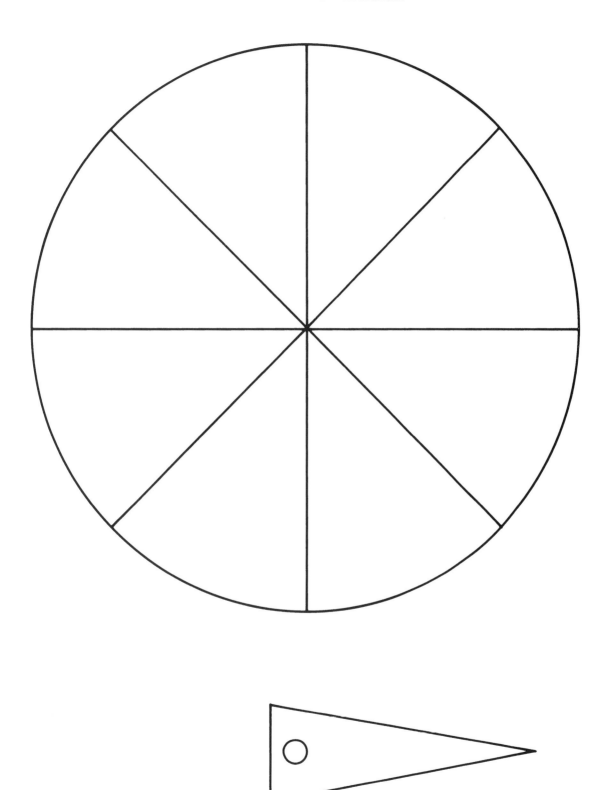

257

Appendix Two

TEACHER NOTES
N-1 THROUGH N-24

TEACHER NOTES (N-1 THROUGH N-24)

N-1 CONNOTATIONS AND DENOTATIONS: A variation is to have you give the words to students that are appropriate for your group, instead of having them look up words. If you have less time or don't have enough dictionaries readily available, give simple words that students will not have to look up. They still can begin to understand the concept of the difference between connotation and denotation while they have fun with this guessing game.

N-2 LETTER COMBOS: This activity is suitable for partnership or small groups as well as individual work.

N-3 DROP AND ADD: These words are taken from third-grade word lists. However, the difficulty level of the puzzle is from 4-6.

N-4 MIXED-UP MARTY (SET I) AND MIXED-UP MARTY (SET II): Several possibilities arise when you have two comparable sets: (1) you might give students who get done early the other set; (2) you might use the sets at different times during the year; (3) you could use one as a practice set, the other as a quiz; (4) some teachers find it a good idea to give a different set to students who are prone to copy (passing out a different set to students sitting next to one another); (5) you can add to the fun by having students do this puzzle in partnerships; and (6) this can be a two-team project, with each team working on a separate set—the first to finish the complete set the winner.

N-5 PLURAL TIC-TAC-TOE: This is just an example for starters. You can easily make other puzzles using words that are group-appropriate to provide lots of practice with plurals, or as noted on the student puzzle sheet, students can make up their own puzzles. The process of making up the puzzles helps students learn a great deal about plurals and which ones are the trickier ones!

N-6 BE PUNNY WITH ADJECTIVES AND NOUNS: This is a great partnership activity. After students get in the mood, the early finishers can think up their own combinations, which are usually pretty amusing.

N-7 BLEEPING THE ADJECTIVES: If you don't want to take the class time needed for students to write their own stories (or want to emphasize adjectives instead of general writing), YOU can read any story or paragraph you choose, say *bleep* where an adjective goes, and have students write their adjectives on their papers. Then reread (or have a student reread) the story pointing to students to fill in the bleeps.

N-8 A CAN OF WORDS: You can use any words you feel are appropriate or words from the following: CANNED SENTENCES GAME (Can 2—Verbs and Can 3—Adverbs); SIMPLIFIED GRAMMAR CARDS (any single word cards—nouns and verbs); WHAT SHAPE ARE YOU IN? (CARDS).

N-9 INITIAL SOUND SENTENCES: These four-letter words are taken from second-grade spelling lists, but can be used with older students as well. Students love to read these sentences aloud to the amusement of their classmates.

N-10 COUPLETS: The verses were attributed to the Odell family of Minneapolis, Minnesota, and over 600 were on roadsides in the United States. Before students write their own couplets, it might be wise to go over poetic rhythm on the chalkboard, using the first example to illustrate the stressed and unstressed syllables with **x** and **/.** Also point out the four "feet" in each line of the couplet.

x /	x /	x /	x /
Within	this vale	of toil	and sin

x /	x /	x /	x /
Your head	grows bald	but not	your chin.

N-11 PARTS OF SPEECH SENTENCE FUN: Usually the sentences are humorous and always give good practice in using parts of speech. There are no winners or losers, just competition for interesting and amusing sentences. If there are not eight students available for one of the teams, just have the last person on the team start over with the first member so that all teams have a full sentence. See N-13 for additional hints on choosing teams fairly.

N-12 ADD ON: If students can't remember the sentences orally, you can modify this game by using the chalkboard. A student can be assigned to write down words as said or you can do it. Another variation is to let students "take notes" at their seats if they want to. Another modification is to read a simple sentence to the students, having them write it down. Then write the sentence again, adding the adjective, still again, adding the adverb, and finally adding the prepositional phrase. Call on students to read their sentences back to you and the class for comments. What method is best depends on the abilities of the group.

N-13 HINTS ON CHOOSING TEAMS: Having students choose teams is risky. Less-able students are not picked to the last and feel left out; students tend to pick their friends, and teams often become unbalanced in skill levels or unruly. Teacher-picked teams are more balanced, but students are sometimes suspicious and resentful having the deck stacked by an adult.

Choosing random teams usually works better. The following simple methods work quickly and effectively: (a) Each student counts and recounts down rows or around tables, depending on number of teams desired (1,2, 1,2 for two teams; 1,2,3,4, 1,2,3,4 for four teams), and students with the same numbers form each team; (b) each row or table is a team; (c) students pull numbers out of a hat or box to see what team they are on.

N-14 COMMON PROVERBS LIST: This list can be used with younger or less-experienced students to help them solve PROVERBS FUN, CODED PROVERBS, PROVERB OPPOSITES, MIXED-UP PROVERBS, PROVERB SQUARES, PROVERB PATHS, PROVERBS BY FIRST LETTERS, PROVERBS BY KEY WORDS, and CAN YOU IDENTIFY THESE PROVERBS? (You would only need to run off a few copies of the first sheet of COMMON PROVERBS LIST for PROVERBS SQUARES, as the proverb is on the first sheet and several students could share the list.)

For students who are older or already have a mental repertoire of proverbs, you might have them try the puzzles without the list and use the list to correct their own papers when finished. Another possibility is to have students study the list of proverbs first, but not allow them to use the list during the puzzle because, in some cases, students could use the number of words or letters given as clues and just scan the list to find the answer without developing any real thinking skills.

A natural follow-up to solving any of the proverb puzzles is to have students write a brief story illustrating the broader meaning of one of their proverb answers.

N-15   CAPITAL FUN: If you are studying social studies and you have maps handy in your text or elsewhere in the room, you may wish to let the students use them for this puzzle.

N-16   SECRET ANIMAL JUMBLE: If you feel the vocabulary of your group is not up to this puzzle, you may wish to write the animal names out of order on the board along with some other animals that are not the correct answers to make the puzzle easier to solve. You could use the following list: sheep, skunk, camel, mouse, bison, tiger, otter, zebra, moose, horse. (The first, fourth, and seventh animals are not among the correct answers, but have the same number of letters.)

N-17   BIRD-O-GRAM: If you feel the vocabulary of your group is not up to this puzzle, you may wish to write the bird names out of order on the board along with some other birds that are not the correct answers to make the puzzle easier to solve. You could use the following list: thrush, magpie, shrike, falcon, pigeon, oriole, phoebe, grouse. (The third, fifth, and sixth birds are not among the correct answers, but have the same number of letters.)

N-18   CARD CATALOG CROSS OUT: Many schools have computerized look-up stations instead of card catalogs to locate books. This game is primarily for schools that use the traditional card catalog system, but it doesn't hurt others, because the principles remain similar.

N-19   SAY WHAT? BETTER USE THE DICTIONARY: This fun sheet can be used either for looking up words in the dictionary or, if desired, students can write out the play on words on the lines. The plays on words are: 1. art study; 2. bury 'em; 3. vowels; 4. Caesar's neighborhood; 5. scanning the area for the cat; 6. die late; 7. enemy; 8. faster; 9. more bid; 10. night rates; 11. "knowed"; 12. patient that is "out" (unconscious); 13. pop's (or pap's) test; 14. Elvis Presley; 15. post (office) operator; 16. wrecked 'em; 17. Caesar; 18. airport terminal; 19. two more; 20. you're in; 21. very close; 22. vanc.

N-20   WORDS THAT CAME FROM VARIOUS COUNTRIES: Supply each pair of students with a dictionary that contains word origins. Before assigning each pair of students one word from the word list, explain that the symbol ≥ means "comes from" and show them where the key to abbreviations of language origins is in the dictionary. Also, be sure to emphasize that they will be trying to translate the language of origin into a probable COUNTRY. That is, if the word came from Old French, the answer would be France.

N-21   NAMES AND THEIR ORIGINS: This might be used in conjunction with or as an introduction to the concept of word origins and etymology.

N-22   ATLAS OR ALMANAC?: Encourage all students to listen while others answer, so they'll learn the correct answers for later when it becomes their turn again or they play the game at another time. The activity could be extended to actually looking up some of the information, but this takes the fun out of the game, and really is not necessary. Students find it quite boring to look up "artificial" information, and it is sometimes best to leave the activity while student interest is high instead of beating it into the ground. See also N-13 for hints on choosing teams.

N-23   HALLOWEEN PUMPKIN: These statements are meant to be very simple. The idea is to differentiate between fact and opinion, not to penalize for lack of reading or comprehension skills, or to be tricky.

N-24   SPINNERS AND MARKERS: See Appendix One for assistance with for easy-to-make spinner patterns. Copy the spinner and spin dial on tagboard and laminate them. If you wish, you could use plastic transparency materials. These methods will result in a more durable and easier-to-use spin dial. Attach spinner to dial with a paper-fastening brad, making sure spinner is free to spin easily. Color with felt pen or use with names of colors on dial.

Suggested markers or tokens for board games: beans, pennies, bottle caps, matches (with fire-ends broken off), shells, toothpicks, stones, beads, poker chips, unshelled nuts. Students can bring in markers. (Bottle tops are especially easy to collect.)

Store the pieces or tokens for board games in see-through plastic baggies with zipper tops. These can be punched with a paper punch so they can be hung on separate nails or hooks in a closet, back of door, or other convenient storage area.

If markers or tokens for board games need to be used, taken off the board, and reused during the game, egg cartons can be sliced to size needed for desired number of categories.

Appendix Three

ANSWER KEY

Section One:
Vocabulary, Spelling, and Word Structure

1-1 SECRET WORD SCRAMBLE: 1. bu(t)ton; 2. pio(n)eer; 3. highw(a)y; 4. arg(u)ment; 5. (s)urprise; 6. p(o)lice; 7. stom(a)ch; 8. chap(t)er; 9. squi(r)rel. *Secret word:* ASTRONAUT.

1-2 DIAMOND IN THE ROUGH (MEDIUM): *Some of the words possible:* hope; rope; cope; lope; core; pore; lore; lose; rose; pose; close; slop; crop; color; school; cool; hero; pooh; posh; pooch; loch; poor; hose; closer; corps; horse; sole; sore; score; loser; corpse; choose; hoop; coop; pool; chore; sore; role; hole; score; shore; pole; shop; slope; sloop; loop. *The nine-letter word:* PRESCHOOL.

1-3 DIAMOND IN THE ROUGH (ADVANCED): *Some of the words possible:* dear; pear; ears; pare; dare; dire; sire; pared; sired; pies; pipe; dipper; dapper; read; reap; rape; sped; spire; paired; aries; ride; side; ripe; appear; pier; pied; spied; sped; spade; paid; spare; spared; spear; parse; sear; parade. *The nine-letter word:* DISAP-PEAR.

1-4 ANIMAWHIRL: 1. bear; 2. rabbit; 3. tiger; 4. rhinoceros; 5. squirrel; 6. leopard; 7. dog; 8. giraffe; 9. elephant.

1-5 VEGGIWHIRL: 1. beet; 2. turnip; 3. pepper; 4. rutabaga; 5. artichoke; 6. eggplant; 7. tomato; 8. okra; 9. asparagus; 10. spinach.

1-6 FORWARD AND REVERSE: *Answers will vary.*

1-7 WORD PYRAMID: 1. eve; 2. edge; 3. erase; 4. edible; 5. educate; 6. eligible; 7. eliminate; 8. exaggerate; 9. expenditure; 10. editorialize; 11. excommunicate; 12. extinguishable.

1-8 IDENTICAL FRONTS AND BACKS: 1. onion; 2. sense; 3. magma; 4. edged; 5. salsa; 6. tomato; 7. eraser; 8. orator; 9. emblem; 10. retire; 11. decode; 12. decide; 13. decade; 14. deride; 15. delude. *Missing letters* (9. bl; 7. as; 10. ti; 2. n; 3. g): *BLASTING.*

1-9 THREE-LETTER WORD BLOCKS: I. (*Across*) mad/ore/pen; (*Down*) mop/are/den. II (*Across*) cot/awe/men; (*Down*) cam/owe/ten.

1-10 FOUR-LETTER WORD BLOCKS: (*Across*) into; roam; once; neon. (*Down*) iron; none; taco; omen.

1-11 ANALOGIES: 1. swim; 2. snout; 3. woman; 4. child; 5. clay; 6. sum; 7. in; 8. sad; 9. math; 10. cow; 11. foot; 12. buck; 13. pumpkin; 14. over; 15. odd; 16. see; 17. fur; 18. laugh; 19. touchdown; 20. five.

1-12 CATS AND RATS: 1. catch; 2. catnap; 3. catsup; 4. catalog; 5. cathedral; 6. scat; 7. bobcat; 8. tomcat; 9. copycat; 10. wildcat; 11. rate; 12. ratio; 13. ration; 14. rattle; 15. rattlesnake; 16. brat; 17. karat or carat; 18. muskrat; 19. democrat; 20. aristocrat.

1-13 GRAPH ROOTS (SET I): 1. autograph; 2. cardiograph; 3. chronograph; 4. cryptograph; 5. electrocardiograph; 6. epigraph; 7. holograph; 8. homograph; 9. mimeograph; 10. monograph; 11. paragraph; 12. phonograph; 13. pictograph; 14. polygraph; 15. seismograph; 16. telegraph.

1-14 GRAPH ROOTS (SET II): 1. autobiography; 2. bibliography; 3. biography; 4. calligraphy; 5. cartography; 6. choreography; 7. cinematography; 8. demography; 9. geography; 10. lexicography; 11. mammography; 12. oceanography; 13. photography; 14. pornography; 15. stenography; 16. topography.

1-15 ARTY WORDS: 1. carton; 2. cartop; 3. barter; 4. garter; 5. farther; 6. partner; 7. cartoon; 8. Martian; 9. charter; 10. quartet; 11. startle; 12. quarter; 13. artist; 14. artery; 15. article; 16. artichoke; 17. arthritis; 18. artificial.

1-16 COMMON CENTS: 1. century; 2. centaur; 3. center; 4. centennial; 5. centipede; 6. accent; 7. ascent; 8. percent; 9. recent; 10. scent.

1-17 VOCAB FUN: 1. anger; 2. limber; 3. learner; 4. rays; 5. ideal; 6. proof; 7. tease; 8. scar; 9. deny; 10. select; 11. weary; 12. theme. *Sentences will vary.*

1-18 NAME THAT SPORT: 1. ceramics (shaping a clay bowl on a potter's wheel); 2. fishing (with artificial bait and a fly rod); 3. using a computer (turning on a computer and bringing the information on the disc to the screen); 4. football (gathering together to inform others of the next play); 5. tennis (love equals zero); 6. ice hockey (taking a penalty because of rough or illegal play); 7. hunting (hunter aims in front of the pheasant or other prey in flight); 8. croquet (missing the metal arch the player was trying to go through); 9. baseball (running to a base safely between pitches); 10. basketball (bouncing the ball); 11. ice hockey (shooting the puck from defensive to offensive territory); 12. knitting (not knitting a stitch to reduce size); 13. golf (putting the ball on the wooden peg before taking the stroke); 14. piano playing (the ivories alluding to the white keys on the piano); 15. horse racing (betting the horse will come in third in the race as opposed to winning or placing second).

1-19 FAMOUS ATHLETES: 1. Griffith-Joyner; 2. Foreman; 3. Evert; 4. Blair; 5. Ryan; 6. Petty; 7. Montana; 8. Gretzky; 9. Bradley; 10. Shoemaker; 11. Evans.

1-20 THINK OF A NAME: *Answers will vary.*

1-21 GUESS WHO OR WHAT I AM: 1. Ford; 2. skunk; 3. Iran; 4. pear; 5. book.

1-22 SYNONYM MATCH: 1. museum; 2. continue; 3. disturb; 4. artist; 5. stomach; 6. cereal; 7. astronaut; 8. gasoline; 9. silent; 10. carpet.

1-23 TOOLS OF THE TRADE: 1. drill; 2. saw; 3. chisel; 4. screwdriver; 5. nails; 6. level; 7. bit; 8. hammer; 9. sawdust; 10. broom.

1-24 CONNOTATIONS AND DENOTATIONS: *Answers will vary.*

1-25 SPIDER SPELLING: *Answers will vary. Some of the words that can be formed:* can; con; don; nod; den; send; case; code; cane; cone; node; codes; nodes; cones; canes; dens; an; as; sand; sane.

1-26 THREE-LETTER WORD CIRCLES AND SQUARES:

c	a	n	o	d
a	o	o	o	o
r	a	t	u	g
a	a	a	a	i
m	a	p	i	n

1-27 THREE PLUS THREE: *Answers may be in any order.* 1. rescue; 2. silent; 3. growth; 4. locate; 5. farmer; 6. supply; 7. polite; 8. arrive; 9. future.

1-28 SPELLING DEMON MAZE: *The following words are misspelled:* 1. cough; 2. neither; 3. balloon; 4. bought; 5. forty; 6. February; 7. laid; 8. loving; 9. several; 10. swimming; 11. tomorrow; 12. we're; 13. you; 14. until; 15. goes.

1-29 WORD BUILDING: 1. day; lady; ready; Monday; holiday; 2. out; auto; pluto; outrun; hideout; 3. try; tray; party; smarty; country; 4. tea; neat; treat; states; wealthy; 5. kit; kite; stick; tickle; kitchen.

1-30 MYSTERY WORDS: 1. net/network; 2. tip/fingertip; 3. but/button; 4. lap/Lapland; 5. dial/sundial; 6. loop/loophole; 7. gum/gumshoe; 8. pin/hairpin; 9. pot/teapot; 10. tool/toolbox.

1-31 IE OR EI: 1. receive; 2. retrieve; 3. belief; 4. neighbor; 5. achieve; 6. alien; 7. deceit; 8. conceive; 9. chief; 10. eight; 11. diesel; 12. quiet; 13. weigh; 14. beige; 15. ceiling; 16. piece; 17. anxiety; 18. brief; 19. perceive; 20. sleigh; 21. vein; 22. veil; 23. reign; 24. rein; 25. pier; 26. ancient; 27. caffeine; 28. neither; 29. counterfeit; 30. either; 31. feisty; 32. forfeit; 33. heir; 34. protein; 35. seize; 36. their; 37. weird.

1-32 LETTER COMBOS: *Answers will vary.*

1-33 WHAT DO WE HAVE IN COMMON?: 1. m; 2. e; 3. f; 4. o; 5. r; 6. d; 7. e. *Scrambled word:* meforde. *Answer:* freedom.

1-34 DROP AND ADD: 1. upper; 2. spare; 3. forge; 4. other; 5. thin; 6. ever/every; 7. boar/oar; 8. late/ate/at/a; 9. lawn; 10. core/ore/or; 11. lash/ash/as/a; 12. slice; 13. omen/men/me; 14. witch; itch; 15. heir.

1-35 ANAGRAM FILL-INS: 1. ten/net; 2. part/trap/tarp; 3. tops/pots/stop/post; 4. seat/eats/teas; 5. heart/earth; 6. teams/mates/steam; 7. pares/pears/spear; 8. beard/bared/bread; 9. stare/tears/rates; 10. alert/later.

1-36 CONFOUNDING COMPOUNDS: 1. long, hair, pin, head, dress (longhair, hairpin, pinhead, headdress); 2. house, hold, up, town, ship, shape (household, holdup, uptown, township, shipshape); 3. over, coat, tail, gate, keeper (overcoat, coattail, tailgate, gatekeeper); 4. news, paper, back, yard, bird, brain (newspaper, paperback, backyard, yardbird, birdbrain); 5. cork, screw, ball, park, way (corkscrew, screwball, ballpark, parkway); 6. gum, drop, out, side, step, brother (gumdrop, dropout, outside, sidestep, stepbrother).

1-37 MIXED-UP MARTY (SET I): 1. airmail; 2. arrowhead; 3. bareback; 4. bulldozer; 5. butterfly; 6. cowboy; 7. cupcake; 8. eggplant; 9. eyeglass; 10. meatloaf; 11. milkshake; 12. toadstool; 13. waterfall; 14. zookeeper.

1-38 MIXED-UP MARTY (SET II): 1. fishhook; 2. football; 3. grasshopper; 4. horseshoe; 5. icebox; 6. jumprope; 7. lawnmower; 8. nightfall; 9. quicksand; 10. quarterback; 11. rattlesnake; 12. shoehorn; 13. tiptoe; 14. wildlife.

1-39 FORWARD AND BACKWARD: 1. may/yam; 2. gum/mug; 3. bus/sub; 4. net/ten; 5. dab/bad; 6. saw/was; 7. Raw/war; 8. rat/tar; 9. top/pot; 10. not/ton; 11. Now/won; 12. but/tub; 13. pal/lap. *Sentences will vary.*

1-40 PREFIX FUN: 1. pare/prepare; 2. amble/preamble; 3. vent/prevent; 4. side/preside; 5. position/preposition; 6. fix/prefix; 7. sent/present; 8. diction/prediction; 9. scribe/prescribe; 10. tend/pretend; 11. face/preface; 12. serve/preserve; 13. tense/pretense.

1-41 SUFFIX FUN: 1. show/shower; 2. snip/sniper; 3. hug/huger; 4. mast/master; 5. add/adder; 6. aft/after; 7. cut/cuter; 8. tow/tower; 9. found/founder; 10. shin/shiner; 11. puck/pucker; 12. plan/planer; 13. box/boxer; 14. cap/caper; 15. pal/paler; 16. corn/corner; 17. sob/sober; 18. cod/coder; 19. cow/cower; 20. row/rower.

1-42 MISSING BRICKS: SUFFIXES: 1. penniless; 2. criticize; 3. running, runner (*any order*); 4. married, marrying (*any order*); 5. dependent, dependence (*any order*); 6. rating, rater (*any order*); 7. prettier, prettiest (*any order*); 8. happiness, happier, happiest (*any order*); 9. attended, attendant, attendance, attending (*any order*).

1-43 MISSING LINKS: SUFFIXES: 1. encouragement; 2. laughable; 3. glamourous; 4. helpful; 5. correction; 6. acreage; 7. quickly; 8. carbonate; 9. mountaineer; 10. handsome.

1-44 DROP DOWN AN AFFIX: (*any order within a category*) 1. underway/subway/midway; 2. tricycle/bicycle/recycle; 3. redo/undo; 4. supercharge/undercharge/discharge; 5. action/acting; actor/active; 6. harmful/harmless/harming; 7. heroism/heroic; 8. attachment/attaching.

1-45 CONTRACTIONS DETECTIVE: 1. o; 2. no; 3. o; 4. o; 5. o; 6. wi (or) sha; 7. woul (or) ha; 8. wi (or) sha; 9. ha; 10. u; 11. woul (or) ha; 12. wi (or) sha; 13. woul (or) ha; 14. wi (or) sha; 15. o; 16. wi (or) sha; 17. ha; 18. ill-o; 19. a; 20. ha. *Mystery message:* now/show/us/how.

1-46 REPEATERS: 1. muumuu (d); 2. tutu (j); 3. mama (c); 4. papa (f); 5. go-go (e); 6. so-so (i); 7. boo-boo (b); 8. bonbon (h); 9. dodo (g); 10. ho ho ho (a). *Picture forms tom-tom.*

1-47 PAIR O' WHAT?: 1. paradise; 2. paradox; 3. parodies; 4. paratroopers; 5. parables; 6. parachutes; 7. paraffins; 8. parakeets; 9. paralyze; 10. parapets; 11. paraphrases; 12. parasites; 13. parasols; 14. paragraphs.

1-48 HOMONYMS: 1. roll/role; 2. loan/lone; 3. soar/sore; 4. vain/vein; 5. flare/flair; 6. cellar/seller; 7. course/coarse; 8. capital/capitol; 9. counsel/council; 10. principal/principle.

1-49 HOOKED-UP HOMONYMS: *Answers will vary.*

1-50 HOMOPHONES: 1. knit; 2. lam; 3. pi; 4. pleas; 5. jamb; 6. inn; 7. aisle; 8. rout; 9. rack; 10. belle; 11. canvas; 12. tease; 13. wrcst.

1-51 HOMOGRAPHS: 1. content; 2. desert; 3. console; 4. bass; 5. does; 6. live; 7. buffet; 8. minute; 9. commune; 10. present; 11. converse; 12. refuse; 13. row; 14. axes; 15. wind; 16. dove; 17. entrance; 18. present; 19. content; 20. dove; 21. axes; 22. converse; 23. bow; 24. entrance; 25. console; 26. intimate; 27. intimate; 28. bass; 29. desert; 30. live; 31. buffet; 32. minute; 33. refuse; 34. commune; 35. row; 36. bow; 37. wind; 38. does.

1-52 PALINDROMES: 1. solos; 2. kayak; 3. stats; 4. madam; 5. radar; 6. sagas; 7. shahs; 8. level; 9. civic; 10. refer; 11. redder.

1-53 PALINDROME CHALLENGE: 1. reviver; 2. repaper; 3. deified; 4. rotator; 5. tenet; 6. deed; 7. Madam, I'm Adam.

1-54 ACRONYMS: MADD MIA: 1. Missing in Action; 2. Mothers Against Drunk Driving; 3. Scholastic Aptitude Test; 4. White Anglo-Saxon Protestant; 5. Personal Identification Number; 6. Special Weapons and Tactics; 7. Mobile Army Surgical Hospital; 8. Political Action Committee; 9. Cost of Living Adjustment; 10. General Agreement on Trade and Tariffs; 11. Cooperative for American Relief Everywhere; 12. National Organization for Women.

1-55 T 4 2: 1. I see you have two eyes; 2. Oh, Arty, I'll owe you. *Made-up sentences will vary.*

1-56 ANAGRAM STEPS: 1. real/learn/nearly; 2. rude/under/refund; 3. rate/later/relate; 4. rote/other/throne; 5. fate/after/falter. *(There may be other solutions.)*

1-57 PLURAL TIC-TAC-TOE: oxen; women; teeth (\).

1-58 WORD SQUARES: *Answers will vary.*

SECTION TWO:
GRAMMAR, PUNCTUATION, AND WRITING

2-1 CHANGING NOUNS WITH S: 1. sport; 2. sash; 3. shoe; 4. spot; 5. soil; 6. sore; 7. switch; 8. sink; 9. score; 10. scent.

2-2 NOUNS: PEOPLE AND THINGS: *Things:* air, bus, checkbook, door, dynamite, elevator, entrance, exit, explosive, fire escape, flame, fumes, gasoline, gate, grass, hands, heat, ice, instruction, poison, post office, property, safety, shelter, station, taxi, time, tunnel, water; *People:* adult, crowd, dentist, doctor, gentlemen, ladies, nurse, pedestrian, police, principal, teacher, violator, waiter. $29 - 13 = 8 + 8 = 16$.

2-3 NOUN/VERB SEARCH: *Possible answers; may be in any order and there may be others.* press; play; talk; joke; time; bend; fax; clear; paper; bone; climb; run; jump; hem; ache; dream; dance; bark.

2-4 BE PUNNY WITH ADJECTIVES AND NOUNS: *Other answers may be possible.* 1. wet pet; 2. frail male; 3. loose goose (or) loose moose; 4. mean bean; 5. road toad; 6. banned sand; 7. tan man; 8. gander dander; 9. bitter sitter; 10. ill Jill; 11. hearty smarty; 12. hen pen; 13. jail tale; 14. rare pair; 15. hot pot; 16. fat cat; 17. lucky ducky; 18. lazy daisy; 19. pink sink; 20. teeny weenie. *Individual puns will vary.*

2-5 ADJECTIVES THAT DESCRIBE ME: *Answers will vary.*

2-6 BLEEPING THE ADJECTIVES: *Stories and adjectives will vary.*

2-7 A CAN OF WORDS: *Answers will vary.*

2-8 PERSONALIZED SENTENCES: *Sentences will vary.*

2-9 DIVIDE AND CONQUER: 1. A noun is the name of a person, place, or thing; 2. Adjectives describe nouns and pronouns; 3. Pronouns can be possessive; 4. A glossary is like a miniature dictionary; 5. Indexes are usually in the backs of books; 6. You use a card catalog to find a book; 7. An encyclopedia is a good reference; 8. Words can be divided into syllables.

2-10 SENTENCE A-MAZE-MENT: 1. What a great day! (exclamatory/emotion); 2. Write the words with your pen. (imperative/command); 3. I did the job. (declarative/statement); 4. Where are you? (interrogative/question).

2-11 DO THESE SENTENCES RING A BELL?: *Connected dots should form a bell.* 1. a (simple); 2. c (compound); 3. f (fragment); 4. h (run-on); 5. j (complex); 6. k (fragment); 7. n (fragment); 8. p (simple); 9. q (run-on); 10. t (run-on); 11. u (compound); 12. x (fragment); 13. y (complex).

2-12 INITIAL SOUND SENTENCES: *Sentences will vary.*

2-13 ALPHABET STORY: *Stories will vary.*

2-14 LIVING STORY: 1. Daisy; 2. Sweet William; 3. poplar; 4. pear; 5. aster; 6. date; 7. Poppy; 8. rose; 9. Sweet William; 10. Daisy; 11. pine; 12. balsam; 13. Paw Paw; 14. palm; 15. fig; 16. four o'clock; 17. Daisy; 18. spruce; 19. beech; 20. gum; 21. Sweet William; 22. tulips; 23. apple; 24. yew; 25. olive.

2-15 MISSING-LETTER STORY: *Missing letter: S; other answers will vary.*

2-16 PROOFREADING CHALLENGES: *Unusual Paragraph:* The paragraph is written without any <u>e</u>'s, the most common vowel in the English language!; *Why Don't I Like Those Things?:* They all have a <u>t</u> in them, and I don't like <u>t</u>.; *The Case of the Missing Letters:* Rubber Baby Buggy Bumpers (missing <u>b</u>); Peter Piper Picked a Peck of Pickled Peppers (missing <u>p</u>).

2-17 LETTER PARTS PUZZLE: *Across:* 3. signature; 5. closing; *Down:* 1. salutation; 2. heading; 4. body.

2-18 USE YOUR IMAGINATION AND PRACTICE PUNCTUATION: *Riddles and punctuation will vary.*

2-19 PUNCTUATION RIDDLES: 1. semi-colon (;); 2. ellipsis (. . .); 3. colon (:); 4. hyphen (-); 5. dash (—); 6. apostrophe ('); 7. italics or underline (___).

2-20 UPDATED NURSERY RHYMES: *Poetry lines will vary.*

2-21 COUPLETS: FIND MY BETTER HALF: *Rhymed answers will vary.*

2-22 COUPLETS: *Original answers will vary.*

2-23 LIMERICKS: WHAT'S MY LINE?: *Last lines will vary.*

2-24 HANG UP A HAIKU: *Each haiku will vary.*

2-29 SIMPLIFIED GRAMMAR: 1. who; 2. how; 3. where; 4. how; 5. who; 6. where; 7. action; 8. how; 9. action; 10. where; 11. what; 12. how; 13. action; 14. what; 15. how; 16. what; 17. what; 18. action; 19. action; 20. where; 21. action; 22. who; 23. what; 24. action; 25. where; 26. who; 27. action; 28. where; 29. what; 30. action; 31. who; 32. action; 33. where; 34. where; 35. how; 36. what; 37. how; 38. how; 39. where; 40. what; 41. what; 42. action; 43. wherc; 44. action; 45. what; 46. how; 47. where; 48. where; 49. how; 50. where.

Section Three: Reading and Literature

3-1 SCATTERGORIZE: *Answers may be in any order under the category. Months:* January, February, March, April, May, June, July, August, September, October, November, December; *Days of Week:* Sunday, Monday, Tuesday, Wednesday, Thursday, Friday, Saturday; *Animals:* alligator, burro, calf, cattle, chipmunk, lamb, monkey, pigeon, pony, squirrel, turkey.

3-2 SAFETY FIRST: *1st column:* 2, 3, 4, 5, 8, 9, 10, 12, 15, 17, 20; *2nd column:* 1, 6, 7, 11, 13, 14, 16, 18, 19. *Both columns add up to 105.*

3-3 IT'S ABOUT TIME: *1st Row Across:* 1, 12, 11, 10; *2nd Row Across:* 12, 11, 10, 9; *3rd Row Across:* 11, 10, 9, 8; *4th Row Across:* 10, 9, 8, 7; *Spelling Grid:* seven, eight, nine, ten, eleven, twelve, one.

3-4 AUTHOR! AUTHOR!: 1. William Shakespeare; 2. *Answers will vary;* 3. Beverly Cleary; 4. *Answers will vary.*

3-5 PSEUDONYMS: 1. Ben Franklin; 2. Charles Dickens; 3. Emily Brontë; 4. Charles Dodgson; 5. Samuel Clemens; 6. Agatha Christie; 7. Cecil Day-Lewis; 8. Charles Lamb; 9. Mary Ann Evans; 10. Eric Blair.

3-6 GO FOR THE GOLD: 1. Silver; 2. Gold; 3. Silver; 4. Silver; 5. Gold; 6. Gold; 7. Silver; 8. Silver; 9. Silver; 10. Bronze; 11. Gold; 12. Gold; 13. Gold; 14. Gold.

3-7 IN BLACK AND WHITE: 1. Black; 2. Black; 3. White; 4. White; 5. Black; 6. Black; 7. Black; 8. Black; 9. White; 10. Black; 11. Black; 12. White; 13. Black; 14. Black; 15. White; 16. White; 17. Black; 18. White; 19. White; 20. Black; 21. Black; 22. White; 23. White.

3-8 READING COUNTS: 1. One; 2. Sixty; 3. 800; 4. 500; 5. Millions; 6. Hundred; 7. One; 8. Two; 9. Three; 10. Dozen; 11. Two; 12. 22; 13. Thirty-Nine; 14. Eighty; 15. 20,000; 16. 1984; 17. 451; 18. Seven; 19. Eight; 20. Seven; 21. Seventeen. *Hints:* 60 + 39 + 1 = 100; 17 − 8 = 7 + 2 (9 = 9); 1 + 3 = 12 - 8 (4 = 4).

3-9 BOOK OR STORY CHARACTERS: 1. Robin Hood from *Robin Hood;* 2. Long John Silver from *Treasure Island;* 3. Alice from *Through the Looking Glass;* 4. Oliver Twist from *Oliver Twist;* 5. Stepmother from *Cinderella;* 6. Dicey from *Dicey's Song;* 7. Miayx from *Julie of the Wolves;* 8. Amos from *Amos Fortune, Free Man.*

3-10 ALL ABOUT BOOKS: 1. writer; 2. illustrator; 3. glossary; 4. publication; 5. title.

3-11 PARTS OF A BOOK: 1. title; 2. spine; 3. cover; 4. contents; 5. index.

3-12 STORY PUZZLE: 1. horse; 2. Alcott; 3. Ramona; 4. pig; 5. Kipling; 6. Harriet; 7. Billy; 8. Twain; 9. grinch; 10. cricket. *Remaining letter message:* THESE STORIES ARE FABULOUS.

3-13 NEWBERY AWARD BOOKS: 1. Sarah, Plain and Tall; 2. The Hero and the Crown; 3. A Gathering of Days; 4. Bridge to Terabithia; 5. The High King; 6. A Wrinkle in Time; 7. Onion John; 8. The Door in the Wall.

3-14 IDIOMS: 1. lend me a hand; 2. drives me crazy; 3. all thumbs; 4. end of my rope; 5. cut corners; 6. nose buried in a book; 7. jumped out of his skin; 8. blew his stack; 9. in the doghouse; 10. on pins and needles; 11. opened a can of worms; 12. trick up his sleeve; 13. splitting headache; 14. tickled pink; 15. cracks me up.

3-15 KNOW YOUR BODY LANGUAGE: 1. head, shoulders; 2. foot; 3. leg; 4. tongue; 5. thumb; 6. teeth; 7. stomach; 8. elbows; 9. eye, eye; 10. face; 11. fingers; 12. throat; 13. toes; 14. nose; 15. knees.

3-16 TEST YOUR LOGIC: Chris (Pittsburgh, Golf, Blue); Maria (New York, Basketball, Green); Babette (San Francisco, Baseball, Yellow); Kendalee (Detroit, Track, Red).

3-18 PROVERBS FUN: 1. r (bird), h (bush); 2. f (flies), y (honey); 3. w (what), p (preach); 4. g (glitters), g (gold); 5. l (loaf), n (none); 6. b (bring); 7. n (never), l (learn); 8. s (skin), 9. l (late), n (never); 10. r (birds), f (flock); 11. e (spite), f (face); 12. s (shoe); 13. s (ship); 14. a (acorns), g (grow); 15. o (good), s (small); 16. c (cart), r (horse); 17. t (twig), g (grow); 18. e (bite), c (chew); 19. n (pan), f (fire); 20. s (sword); 21. f (fair), p (play); 22. n (never), b (boils); 23. s (shuts), o (opens); 24. p (place), p (place); 25. s (speak).

3-19 PROVERBS BY FIRST LETTERS: 1. A penny saved is a penny earned; 2. If at first you don't succeed, try, try again; 3. Out of the frying pan, into the fire; 4. Talk is cheap; 5. Don't cry over spilt milk; 6. Don't try to lock the barn after the horses are stolen; 7. Handsome is as handsome does.

3-20 CODED PROVERBS: 1. A good book is the best companion (/ stands for each letter); 2. Absence makes the heart grow fonder (V = Vowel; C = Consonant); 3. All's well that ends well (Each letter is one preceding the one given in the alphabet); 4. Where there's smoke, there's fire (Each _ stands for a letter); 5. It takes a thief to know one (Each square stands for a letter; each / stands for end of word); 6. A stitch in time saves nine (Divide letters into words); 7. Paddle your own canoe (Unscramble the letters).

3-21 PROVERB OPPOSITES: *Most obvious from the list are:* 1. He who hesitates is lost/Look before you leap; 2. Don't cross the bridge before you come to it/Forewarned is forearmed; 3. Birds of a feather flock together/Opposites attract; 4. Too many cooks spoil the broth/Two heads are better than one; 5. The pen is

275

mightier than the sword/Actions speak louder than words. *Others might include:* You're never too old to learn/You can't teach an old dog new tricks; Variety is the spice of life/Don't change horses in the middle of the stream; The squeaky wheel gets the grease/Silence is golden.

3-22 MIXED-UP PROVERBS: 1. One man's meat is another man's poison/An ounce of prevention is worth a pound of cure; 2. Lie down with dogs; get up with fleas/When the cat's away, the mice will play; 3. A rotten apple spoils the barrel/The early bird catches the worm; 4. Fools rush in where angels fear to tread/Don't count your chickens before they're hatched; 5. Misery loves company/A fool and his money are soon parted; 6. Every rose has its thorn/Every cloud has a silver lining; 7. You can't have your cake and eat it, too/You make your bed; you must lie on it.

3-23 PROVERB SQUARES:

A	///	B	I	R	D	///	I	N	///	T
H	E	///	H	A	N	D	///	I	S	///
W	O	R	T	H	///	T	W	O	///	I
N	///	T	H	E	///	B	U	S	H	///

Proverb: A bird in the hand is worth two in the bush.

3-24 PROVERB PATHS: 1. Look before you leap; 2. Overcome evil with good.

1.

2.

3-25 PROVERBS BY KEY WORDS: *Capitalized words are key words.* 1. Don't rob PETER to pay Paul; 2. EASY come, EASY go; 3. He who HESITATES is lost; 4. JACK of all trades, master of one; 5. NOTHING ventured, NOTHING gained; 6. Never make a mountain out of a MOLEHILL; 7. Too many COOKS spoil the broth.

3-26 CAN YOU IDENTIFY THESE PROVERBS?: 1. Don't cry over spilt milk; 2. Cleanliness is next to godliness; 3. A stitch in time saves nine; 4. Blood is thicker than water; 5. Two heads are better than one; 6. Don't put all your eggs in one basket; 7. Every rose has its thorn.

SECTION FOUR:
OTHER CONTENT AREAS

Social Studies

4-1 FAMOUS PLACES: 1. C; 2. G; 3. J; 4. A; 5. M; 6. L; 7. E; 8. D; 9. F; 10. B; 11. H; 12. I; 13. K. *Shaded Shape:* house.

4-2 ALPHA CHALLENGE: *Group I:* Albany, Annapolis, Atlanta, Augusta, Austin; *Group II:* Sacramento, St. Paul, Salem, Salt Lake City, Santa Fe, Springfield; *Group III:* Baton Rouge, Bismarck, Boise, Boston; *Group IV:* Carson City, Charleston, Cheyenne, Columbia, Columbus, Concord.

4-3 CAPITAL FUN: 1. MONT GOM ER Y: 2. JU NEAU; 3. PHOE NIX; 4. DEN VER; 5. HART FORD; 6. TAL LA HAS SEE; 7. HON O LU LU; 8. IN DI AN AP O LIS; 9. DES MOINES; 10. TO PE KA; 11. FRANK FORT; 12. LAN SING; 13. JACK SON; 14. LIN COLN; 15. TREN TON; 16. RA LEIGH; 17. HAR RIS BURG; 18. PROV I DENCE; 19. PI ERRE; 20. NASH VILLE; 21. MONT PEL IER; 22. RICH MOND; 23. O LYM PI A; 24. MAD I SON.

4-4 CITIES AROUND THE WORLD: *Across:* 2. Turkey; 3. Taiwan; 5. Japan; 8. Iraq; 9. Argentina; 12. Mexico; 14. Russia; 16. Australia; 17. France. *Down:* 1. Brazil; 2. Thailand; 4. India; 6. China; 7. United States; 10. Portugal; 11. Germany; 13. Italy; 15. Spain.

4-5 ROUNDABOUTS: *Set 1:* Washington, Wisconsin, California; *Set 2:* Yugoslavia, United States, Antarctica; *Set 3:* superintendent, oceanographer, cardiologist.

4-6 A STATE BY ANY OTHER NAME: 1. Alaska; 2. Arkansas; 3. Colorado; 4. Hawaii; 5. Illinois; 6. Iowa; 7. Louisiana; 8. Mississippi; 9. Montana; 10. New Hampshire; 11. New Mexico; 12. North Dakota; 13. Oklahoma; 14. Pennsylvania; 15. Tennessee; 16. Utah; 17. Virginia; 18. Washington; 19. Wisconsin; 20. Wyoming.

4-7 NAME THAT STATE: *Across:* 5. Florida; 8. Arizona; 10. Iowa; 11. Oregon; 13. Indiana; 14. Kansas; 15. New Jersey. *Down:* 1. Idaho; 2. California; 3. Texas; 4. Vermont; 6. Ohio; 7. Nebraska; 9. New York; 12. Maine.

4-8 HAVING FUN WITH STATE ABBREVIATIONS (I): 1. alms; 2. arid; 3. cain; 4. code; 5. deal; 6. flak; 7. gain; 8. hide; 9. inca; 10. lade; 11. meal; 12. maid; 13. mime; 14. moms; 15. near; 16. oral; 17. pail; 18. rind; 19. scar; 20. vain; 21. wade; 22. wine; 23. wind.

4-9 HAVING FUN WITH STATE ABBREVIATIONS (II): 1. alar; 2. aria; 3. came; 4. coil; 5. dear; 6. gala; 7. game; 8. laid; 9. lain; 10. mega; 11. mane; 12. mica; 13. mode; 14. paid; 15. pain; 16. pane; 17. rime; 18. rims; 19. vane; 20. wail; 21. wane; 22. wand; 23. wide.

4-10 HAVING FUN WITH STATE ABBREVIATIONS (III): 1. arks; 2. arms; 3. cams; 4. cane; 5. coal; 6. coin; 7. cola; 8. come; 9. coma; 10. cone; 11. demi; 12. demo; 13. gams; 14. lame; 15. lane; 16. lava; 17. memo; 18. mend; 19. made; 20. mail; 21. main; 22. mine; 23. ride.

4-11 CUT-OFF COMMUNICATION: *List can be in any order.* Morse code; modem; videotape; record; letter; computer; sign language; CD-ROM; disc; television; telephone; body language; fax machine; telegraph; newspaper; magazine; typewriter.

4-12 GETTING THERE IS HALF THE FUN: *Code numbers that should be shaded are forms of transportation:* 2a. automobile; 2b. helicopter; 2d. horse; 3a. motorcycle; 3b. bicycle; 3c. skateboard; 3d. ship; 4a. locomotive; 4b. submarine; 4c. surfboard; 4d. snowmobile; 5a. snowshoes; 5b. roller blades; 5c. ice skates; 7d. airplane; 8c. bus; 8d. taxi; 9c. escalator; 9d. elevator; 10c. wheelchair; 10d. cable car; 11c. truck; 11d. stilts; 12c. moped. *The shaded areas and lines drawn should form a* SAILBOAT.

4-13 JOB-RELATED NAMES: *Answers will vary. Some possibilities:* Butcher; Baker; Carpenter; Taylor (Tailor); Smith (Blacksmith); Weaver; Alderman; Merchant; King; Hammer; Fisher; Hunter; Plummer (Plumber); Cooper; Porter; Stoner; Stockman; Weber; Troutman; Kohlman (Coalman); Cotton; Chaplin (Chaplain); Farmer; Church; Churchman; Clay; Cleaver; Brand; Bowler; Bower; Berger; Beer; Berry; Wolfman; Wolf; Woodman; Miller; Miner; Marker; Lynch; Law; Lawson; Last; Lamb; Lackey; Clark (Clerk); Brewer; Boxer; Bowman.

4-14 BUILD A CAREER: 1. preacher; 2. police; 3. fireman; 4. roofer; 5. barber; 6. lawyer; 7. doctor; 8. mechanic; 9. grocer; 10. druggist; 11. waitress; 12. butcher; 13. singer; 14. clerk.

4-15 FLAG IDENTIFICATION: 1. Japan; 2. Somalia; 3. Switzerland; 4. France; 5. Italy; 6. Rwanda; 7. South Africa; 8. Libya; 9. Vietnam; 10. Canada.

4-16 PRESIDENTS: 1. 6; 2. 6; 3. 4; 4. John F. Kennedy; 5. 8; 6. 7; 7. Abraham Lincoln; 8. Franklin Roosevelt; 9. William Clinton.

Science

4-17 SECRET ANIMAL JUMBLE: 1. camel; 2. zebra; 3. horse; 4. tiger; 5. bison; 6. moose; 7. skunk. *Secret animal:* CARIBOU.

4-18 CHEWING THE CUD: 1. giraffe (2); 2. zebu (2); 3. buffalo (3); 4. ox (1); 5. addax (2); 6. camel (2); 7. impala (3); 8. gnu (1); 9. goat (1); 10. eland (2); 11. deer (1); 12. gazelle (2); 13. yak (1); 14. bongo (2); 15. oryx (2); 16. caribou (3); 17. ibex (2); 18. moose (1); 19. kudu (2); 20. wapiti (3). *There are 19 syllables in each column.*

4-19 THE MALE OF THE SPECIES: 1. dog; 2. bull; 3. billy; 4. jack; 5. buck; 6. stallion; 7. boar.

4-20 WILD CATS: 1. leopard; 2. ocelot; 3. lynx; 4. lion; 5. tiger; 6. bobcat; 7. cougar; 8. jaguar; 9. caracal; 10. cheetah. *Advice:* Do not touch.

4-21 GOING TO THE DOGS: *Answers can be in any order within a set. Beginning with D:* Dachshund; Dalmatian. *Two syllables:* Collie; Setter; Pointer; Schnauzer; Beagle; Griffon; Spaniel; Sheepdog; Great Dane; Mastiff; Pinscher; Poodle; Bulldog; Chow Chow. *Rhymes:* Husky. *Backwards:* Papillon. *Repeated syllables:* Chow Chow; Chihuahua.

4-22 SECRET BIRD JUMBLE: 1. robin; 2. grebe; 3. finch; 4. goose; 5. eagle; 6. snipe. *Secret bird:* ORIOLE.

4-23 BIRD-O-GRAM: 1. phoebe; 2. falcon; 3. thrush; 4. grouse; 5. magpie. *It is possible for students to figure out other words and their scores should be added appropriately.*

4-24 BIRD COLORS: 1. Black (Duck); 2. Blue (Goose); 3. (Bob)white; 4. Red (-Headed Woodpecker) *Note: There is also a White-Headed Woodpecker;* 5. Yellow (-Bellied Sapsucker); 6. Purple (Martin); 7. Blue (Jay) *Note: There are also Green Jays and Grey Jays but not in BIRD COLORS list;* 8. Black(bird) *Note: There are also Bluebirds and Redbirds;* 9. Scarlet (Tanager); 10. Red(-Winged Blackbird).

4-25 PLANT RINGS: 1. carnation; 2. periwinkle; 3. gardenia; 4. violet; 5. feverfew; 6. avocado; 7. pepper; 8. piggyback. *Last letters:* WORK.

4-26 POISONOUS PLANTS: *1 through 6 in any order:* 1. oi (castor-oil); 2. ph (delphinium); 3. ck (hemlock); 4. au (laurel); 5. sh (mushroom); 6. rh (rhubarb); *7 through 17 in any order:* 7. tt (nettle); 8. nn (fennel); 9. ll (belladonna); 10. nn (belladonna); 11. tt (bittersweet); 12. ee (bittersweet); 13. ll (hellebore); 14. ll (holly); 15. ee (locoweed); 16. oo (mushroom); 17. ee (pokeweed).

4-27 FRUIT LOOPS: *Across:* lemon, apricot, grape, fig, peach, cherry, plum, apple, lime, raisin, pear, melon. *Down:* banana, orange, pineapple, tangerine.

4-28 LET'S GO ANGLING:

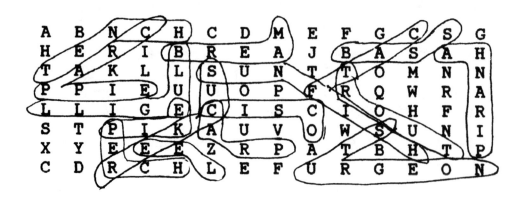

4-29 SOMETHING BUGGING YOU?: 1. cricket; 2. firefly; 3. ladybug; 4. katydid; 5. termite; 6. mealybug; 7. gall wasp; 8. stinkbug; 9. honeybee; 10. housefly. *What you need:* FLY SWATTER.

4-30 ANATOMY: 1. i; 2. y; 3. h; 4. none; 5. e; 6. e; 7. e; 8. e; 9. h; 10. e; 11. none; 12. l/d/e. *Across:* gall (gallbladder); hear (heart); live (liver); *Down:* ache (trachea); rain (brain); test (intestine).

4-31 JEWELS AND GEMS: *Green:* 1. bloodstone; 2. emerald; 3. jade; 4. olivine; 5. peridot. *Red:* 1. carnelian; 2. garnet; 3. ruby. *Yellow:* 1. amber; 2. citrine; 3. topaz. *White:* 1. moonstone; 2. pearl. *Blue:* 1. aquamarine; 2. lapis lazuli; 3. sapphire; 4. turquoise. *Miscellaneous:* 1. amethyst; 2. diamond; 3. onyx (*These are purple, clear, and black respectively and it might be deduced that they are a different category because of the double letters in their stock code numbers. All code numbers use the first letter of the color of the gem.*)

4-32 ORES AND MINERALS: *Any order within categories. One syllable:* coal; gold; quartz; talc. *Two syllables:* barite; bismuth; calcite; copper; gypsum; lignite, pyrite; silver; stibnite; sulfur. *Three syllables:* corundum; galena; hematite; lazulite; magnetite; platinum.

Mathematics

4-33 PROGRESSIONS:

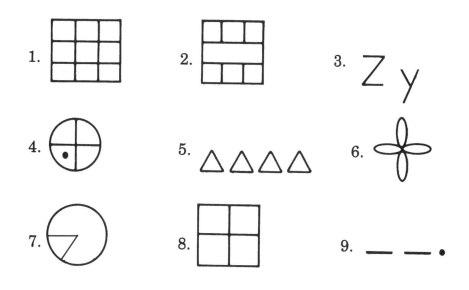

10. **H**

4-34 ZIGZAG MATH SEARCH:

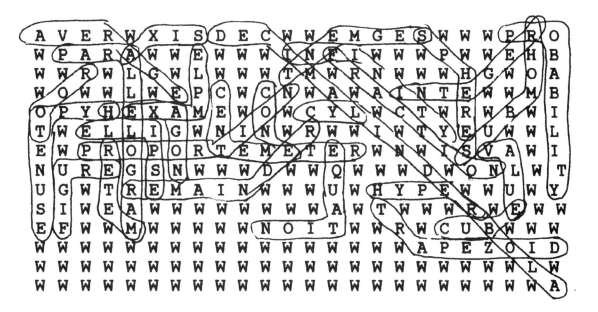

4-35 MATH VOCABULARY SYMBOLS: 1. T; 2. T; 3. F; 4. F; 5. T; 6. T; 7. T; 8. F; 9. T; 10. F; 11. T; 12. T. *Statement:* Number true minus number false equals 4.

4-36 MATH VOCABULARY MUDDLE: *Words read across from top to bottom:* sum, product, multiply, square, triangle, add, difference, quotient, divide, subtract, circle, rectangle.

4-37 MONTH MATH: 1. September, 9, May, 3, 9 + 3 = 12; 2. February, November, December, $3 \times 8 = 2 \times 12$ (24 = 24); 3. 4 + 4 + 2 = 5 + 5 (10 = 10); 4. $7 \times 7 = 9 + 40$ (49 = 49); 5. $4 \times 6 = 8 \times 3$ (24 = 24).

4-38 MATH SQUARES:

#1

4	+	5	÷	3	= 3
+	▨	−	▨	x	▨
4	x	1	+	2	= 6
−	▨	x	▨	÷	▨
2	x	2	−	3	= 1
= 6	▨	= 8	▨	= 2	▨

#2

16	+	4	÷	5	= 4
+	▨	x	▨	−	▨
2	÷	2	x	2	= 2
÷	▨	−	▨	x	▨
3	+	1	÷	4	= 1
= 6	▨	= 7	▨	= 12	▨

4-39 CAN YOU MAKE CENTS?: 1. 1; 2. 5; 3. 10; 4. 25; 5. 50; 6. 100; 7. 5 cents; 8. 11 cents; 9. 25 cents; 10. zero or nothing; 11. 65 cents.

4-40 NUMBERS COUNT: 1. 21; 2. 7; 3. 10; 4. 12; 5. 14; 6. 12; *(total 1-6 = 76)*; 7. 32; 8. 13; 9. 12; 10. 8; 11. 5; 12. 6; *(total 7-12 = 76)*; 13. 76; 14. 76; 15. 76.

4-41 HOW DO YOU MEASURE UP?: 1. S (lumber); 2. J (timepiece); 3. R (shoes); 4. I (light bulb); 5. O (tire); 6. B (fuse); 7. C (film); 8. F (rifle); 9. P (gold); 10. H (shirt/male); 11. D (clothes/baby); 12. N (motor); 13. Q (batteries); 14. E (clothes/female); 15. L (nails); 16. A (temperature fahrenheit); 17. G (computer memory in thousands of kilobytes); 18. K (metric length in decimeters); 19. T (liquid capacity in ounces); 20. M (visual acuity).

4-42 ROMAN NUMERAL FUN: 1. MODEL; 2. DOME; 3. VIXEN; 4. VILE; 5. VIM; 6. MIDDLE; 7. MOVIE; 8. VIDEO; 9. LIVID; 10. TAXI; 11. X-RAY; 12. VIOLET; 13. DIVE; 14. CIVIL; 15. EXIT; 16. CODE; 17. DIVIDE; 18. MILL.

4-43 WORLD CURRENCIES: 1. yen; 2. dollar; 3. lira; 4. dinar; 5. rupee; 6. mark; 7. yuan; 8. peso; 9. franc; 10. rand; 11. peseta; 12. krona; 13. pound.

4-44 GEOMETRIC SHAPES: 1. square; 2. octagon; 3. triangle; 4. ellipse; 5. circle; 6. rectangle; 7. pentagon; 8. hexagon.

The Arts

4-46 SOUNDS OF MUSIC: *Across:* 3. forte; 7. soprano; 9. metronome; 10. falsetto; 11. chord; 12. duct; 14. note; 16. harmony. *Down:* 1. tempo; 2. quartet; 3. fret; 4. ensemble; 5. staff; 6. contralto; 8. octave; 9. melody; 11. coda; 13. triad; 15. tenor.

4-47 SCRAMBLED MUSIC FORMS: 1. anthem; 2. aria; 3. ballad; 4. cantata; 5. concerto; 6. fugue; 7. madrigal; 8. minuet; 9. nocturne; 10. overture; 11. prelude; 12. quartet; 13. rhapsody; 14. round; 15. sonata.

4-48 MUSICAL TEASE: *These words should be shaded or colored:* xylophone, chimes, bells, gong, glockenspiel, cymbals, triangle. *The names used for the major percussion instrument are KETTLEDRUMS and TIMPANI.*

4-49 ORCHESTRA PIT: 1. bass viol; 2. bassoon; 3. cello; 4. clarinet; 5. cornet; 6. English horn; 7. harp; 8. oboe; 9. piccolo; 10. sousaphone; 11. trombone; 12. timpani; 13. tuba.

4-50 ANCIENT INSTRUMENTS: *Words read across from top to bottom:* timpani, harp, viol, violin, cello, organ, bagpipe, piano, recorder.

4-51 NATIVE AMERICAN DANCES (SET I): 1. long-house; 2. ghost; 3. corn; 4. sun; 5. swan; 6. potlatch; 7. deer; 8. mime.

4-52 NATIVE AMERICAN DANCES (SET II): 1. war; 2. stomp; 3. snake; 4. story; 5. green corn; 6. turkey; 7. butterfly; 8. basket.

4-53 AFRICAN-AMERICAN INFLUENCE ON MUSIC AND DANCE: 1. jazz; 2. bebop; 3. blues; 4. rap; 5. hip hop; 6. boogie; 7. shimmy.

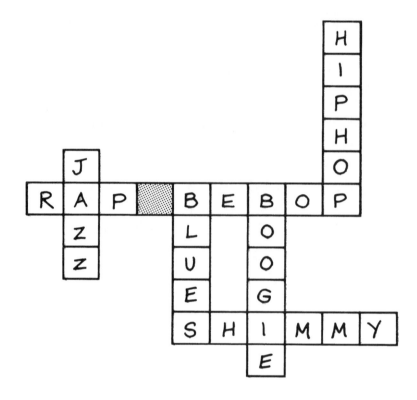

4-54 SPANISH AND LATINO INFLUENCE ON MUSIC AND DANCE: 1. conga; 2. rumba; 3. samba; 4. cha cha; 5. salsa; 6. calypso; 7. tango.

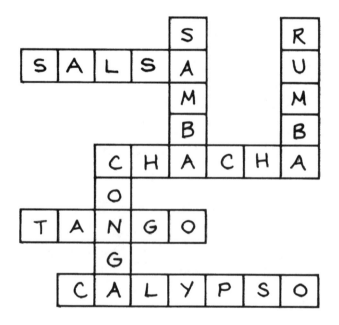

4-55 DECODE THE BALLET: 1. adagio; 2. arabesque; 3. cabriole; 4. elevation; 5. leotard; 6. jete; 7. plie; 8. pointe; 9. positions; 10. tutu.

4-56 COLOR ME RED: *Shaded boxes:* 1-2-3-4-6-8-10-12-14-16-17-18-19-20. *Shaded area should form a* **D,** *the last letter in the color* **red.**

4-57 PAINTING STYLES: 1. abstract; 2. baroque; 3. impressionism; 4. renaissance; 5. fauvism; 6. dadaism; 7. mannerism; 8. futurism; 9. realism; 10. action; 11. cubism; 12. neoclassicism; 13. expressionism; 14. surrealism; 15. postimpressionism.

4-58 LIGHTS! CAMERA! ACTION!: 1. director; 2. Action; 3. actresses; 4. actors (*numbers 3 and 4 can be reversed*); 5. stage; 6. audience; 7. curtain; 8. play; 9. character; 10. entrance; 11. costume; 12; makeup; 13. disguise; 14. stagehand; 15. scenery; 16. set (*numbers 15 and 16 can be reversed*); 17. cast; 18. house; 19. downstage; 20. curtain call; 21. rehearsed; 22. playwright; 23. dialog; 24. script; 25. lines; 26. cues; 27. prompter; 28. exit; 29. theater; 30. tragedy; 31. comedy (*numbers 30 and 31 can be reversed*).

4-59 ADDITION AND SUBTRACTION: 1. drama; 2. costume; 3. actor; 4. rehearse; 5. comedy; 6. scenery; 7. actress; 8. stage; 9. property; 10. tragedy. *Words are related to:* THEATER.

4-60 THE PLAY'S THE THING: *Across:* props; arena; actor; backstage; costumes; flies; stage; playwright. *Down:* proscenium; set; crew; producer; director; scene.

SECTION FIVE: LIBRARY AND REFERENCE

5-1 CARD CATALOG CROSS OUT: *Top of Page:* LIBRARY; 1. subject (drawer E); 2. author (drawer MN-MZ); 3. title (drawer G); 4. author (drawer H); 5. subject (drawer D); 6. title (drawer FN-FZ); 7. subject (drawer Y-Z); 8. title (drawer S-SM); 9. author (drawer F-FM).

5-2 LIBRARY SKILLS REVIEW: 1. E; 2. N; 3. J; 4. O; 5. Y; 6. T; 7. H; 8. E; 9. L; 10. I; 11. B; 12. R; 13. A; 14. R; 15. Y. *Secret Message:* ENJOY THE LIBRARY.

5-3 MORSE CODE LIBRARY TERMS: 1. title; 2. author; 3. subject; 4. computer search; 5. card catalog; 6. Dewey Decimal System.

5-4 DEWEY DECIMAL SUBCATEGORIES: *500-599 (Pure Science):* 2, 7, 8, 10, 13; *600-699 (Technology):* 3, 4, 6, 12, 15; *700-799 (The Arts):* 1, 5, 9, 11, 14.

5-5 BIOGRAPHIES: 6, 5; 2, 9; 10, 1; 8, 3; 4, 7. (*Each pair equals 11.*)

5-6 ENCYCLOPEDIA TOPICS: 1. fish; 2. cat; 3. snake; 4. animal; 5. baseball; 6. horse; 7. dinosaur; 8. dog; 9. president; 10. bird. *First:* ANIMAL; *Last:* SNAKE.

5-7 SEE ALSO: 1. E; 2. X; 3. C; 4. E; 5. L; 6. L; 7. E; 8. N; 9. T. *Word spelled downward:* EXCELLENT.

5-8 SAY WHAT? BETTER CHECK THE DICTIONARY!: *Definitions:* 1. blood tube; 2. chemical; 3. intestines; 4. diagnostic test; 5. burn off unwanted tissue; 6. open up; 7. injection of liquid to purge intestines; 8. to form pus; 9. gruesome; diseased; 10. nitric acids; 11. knot; swelling; 12. person getting treated outside of hospital; 13. test for uterine cancer; 14. area between hip bones; 15. after an operation; 16. lower segment of intestines; 17. sudden attack of disease; 18. at the final stages of an illness; 19. growth; 20. waste liquid; 21. very swollen; 22. blood vessel. *See N-10 for plays on words.*

5-9 WORDS THAT CAME FROM PEOPLE: 1. braille; 2. boycott; 3. Mae West (life preserver); 4. bloomers; 5. shaddock; 6. maverick; 7. sandwich; 8. knickers; 9. saxophone; 10. pasteurize.

5-10 WORDS THAT CAME FROM VARIOUS COUNTRIES: 1. Germany; 2. Greece; 3. Rome; 4. France; 5. Italy; 6. Spain; 7. China; 8. France; 9. Russia; 10. Japan; 11. America (Algonquian); 12. Persia; 13. Israel; 14. America (Eskimo); 15. Africa.

5-13 DEWEY DECIMAL REVIEW: *Correct card order:* Card 1 (841); Card 2 (841.25); Card 3 (841.26); Card 4 (841.28); Card 5 (841.283); Card 6 (841.288); Card 7 (841.3); Card 8 (842).

5-15 ATLAS OR ALMANAC? *Answers to the following questions are best located in an almanac:* 1. Who won the World Series in 1990? 2. How many motorcycles are in the United States? 3. What is the average price that farmers receive for beef? 4. Who is the mayor of San Francisco? 5. Who are the senators from your state? 6. When did your state enter the union? 7. Who was Miss America in 1926? 8. What actor won the Oscar for best picture in 1995? 9. How does the population of your state compare with the other states? 10. Who was MVP in the Super Bowl in 1994? 11. What is the capacity of the Metrodome in Minneapolis? 12. How did your state vote in the last major presidential election? 13. What amendment to the Constitution lowers the voting age to 18? 14. Who signed the Declaration of Independence? 15. Who was the wife of former President Truman? 16. Who won the first Kentucky Derby in 1875? 17. Who was NBA Rookie of the Year in 1979? 18. What is the biggest freshwater fish ever caught? 19. Who was the heavyweight champion of the world from 1974-1977? 20. Who won the major League Baseball Pennant in 1901?

Answers to the following questions are best located in an atlas: 1. How far is it from Chicago to Des Moines? 2. On what continent is Tanzania? 3. What states border your state? 4. Is there a road from Detroit to Mackinac Island, Michigan? 5. Is Corpus Christi on the Gulf of Mexico? 6. What is your state shaped like? 7. Does India border China? 8. How many provinces are there in Canada? 9. Which states have a common border with Mexico? 10. Where is the largest country in South America located? 11. Is Japan an island or a series of islands? 12. What are the latitude and longitude of Mongolia? 13. What countries have a coastline on the

Mediterranean Sea? 14. Where is Iraq? 15. Is Ireland part of England? 16. How many continents are there? 17. Which states have Pacific Ocean coastlines? 18. Which state is almost surrounded by large, freshwater lakes? 19. How far is it from Florida to North Dakota? 20. Where is the major river in Nebraska located?

SECTION SIX:
HOLIDAYS AND SEASONS

6-1 HOLIDAY CODES: 1. Christmas; 2. George Washington; 3. January; 4. St. Patrick's; 5. Groundhog; 6. June; 7. November; 8. Hanukkah; 9. Martin Luther King; 10. fourth.

6-2 OCTOBER DAZE: 1. back; 2. *drawings will vary;* 3. Christopher; 4. People of the Jewish faith.

O	C	T	O	B	E	R
S	**M**	**T**	**W**	**T**	**F**	**S**
1	**2**	**3** 1995 Yom Kippur at sundown	**4**	**5**	**6**	**7**
8	**9** 1995 Columbus Day	**10**	**11**	**12**	**13**	**14**
15	**16**	**17**	**18**	**19**	**20**	**21**
22 Daylight Savings ends	**23**	**24**	**25**	**26**	**27**	**28**
29	**30**	**31** Halloween				

6-3 HALLOWEEN PUMPKIN: 1. F; 2. F; 3. O; 4. F; 5. O; 6. F; 7. O; 8. F; 9. F; 10. F; 11. F; 12. O. *Numbers 1/2/4/6/8/9/10/11 should be connected forming a roughly round image. Pumpkin faces will vary.*

6-4 SPECIAL NOVEMBER DAYS: *Answers will vary depending on age and level of pupils. Possible answers:* **Thanksgiving:** food, turkey, cranberries, corn, pie, prayer, pilgrims, church, Indians, Native Americans, harvest, feast; **Veterans Day:** servicemen and women, Army, Navy, Marines, veterans, war, guns, ships, death, Vietnam Memorial, Tomb of the Unknown Soldier, flags, salute, prayer, peace; **Election Day:** vote, Republican, Democrat, Independent, voting machine, ballot, fraud, rights, responsibility, duty, winner, loser, recount, flags, President, mayor, Congress, Senate, House of Representatives.

6-5 DECEMBER DAYS OUTLINE: *Main topics I, II, and V must be as shown below because of the number of subtopics. Main topics III and IV are interchangeable. All subheadings can be in any order as long as they are placed under the correct main topic. Probable outline:*

I. Christmas Day
   A. December 25
   B. Presents
   C. Christian celebration
   D. Birth of Christ
   E. Santa Claus
   F. Evergreen trees
II. Hanukkah
   A. December (usually)
   B. Jewish festival
   C. Rededication of Temple
   D. 8-day celebration
   E. Menorah

III. Pearl Harbor Day
   A. December 7
   B. Japanese bombing of Hawaii
   C. Year of 1941
IV. Official End of WWII
   A. December 31
   B. Defeat of the Axis
   C. Year of 1946
V. First Day of Winter
   A. December 21
   B. Winter solstice (U.S.)
   C. Shortest day (U.S.)
   D. Colder weather

There is a legitimate argument to be made over some of the main topics. For example, perhaps **Winter Solstice (U.S.)** *would make as good a main heading as* **First Day of Winter.** *(Calendars designate this either way.) A little leeway should be allowed.*

6-6 WINTERTIME FUN: *Drawing should look like a snowman with hat and scarf. Holly should decorate the hat and the bottom of the picture.*

6-7 BROKEN HEARTS OF ART: 1. cathe/dral (c); 2. eas/el (e); 3. mur/al (a); 4. sculp/ture (i); 5. perspec/tive (b); 6. sp/ace (k); 7. water/color (j); 8. car/ving (h); 9. fres/co (l); 10. can/vas (d); 11. pain/ting (f); 12. temp/era (g).

6-8 ST. PATRICK'S DAY WORDS: 1. s (Ireland); 2. h (green); 3. a (emerald); 4. m (shamrock); 5. r (Boston); 6. o (March 17); 7. c (3); 8. k (missionary). *Symbol of holiday:* SHAMROCK.

6-9 EASTER "EGGS:" 1. exact; 2. exam; 3. example; 4. examine; 5. excavate; 6. extra; 7. excellent; 8. exchange; 9. excite; 10. excuse; 11. execute; 12. exercise; 13. exhaust; 14. exile; 15. expire.